Strategies for the Professional Leader

PEER POWER

BOOK TWO

Strategies for the Professional Leader
Applying Peer Helper Skills

PEER POWER

BOOK TWO

THIRD EDITION

Judith A. Tindall, Ph.D.

Routledge
Taylor & Francis Group
New York   London

Routledge
Taylor & Francis Group
270 Madison Avenue
New York, NY 10016

Routledge
Taylor & Francis Group
2 Park Square
Milton Park, Abingdon
Oxon OX14 4RN

© 2009 by Taylor & Francis Group, LLC
Routledge is an imprint of Taylor & Francis Group, an Informa business

Printed in the United States of America on acid-free paper
10 9 8 7 6 5 4 3 2 1

International Standard Book Number-13: 978-0-415-96233-9 (Softcover)

Except as permitted under U.S. Copyright Law, no part of this book may be reprinted, reproduced, transmitted, or utilized in any form by any electronic, mechanical, or other means, now known or hereafter invented, including photocopying, microfilming, and recording, or in any information storage or retrieval system, without written permission from the publishers.

Trademark Notice: Product or corporate names may be trademarks or registered trademarks, and are used only for identification and explanation without intent to infringe.

Library of Congress Cataloging-in-Publication Data

Tindall, Judith A., 1942-
  Peer power, book two : strategies for the professional leader : applying peer helper skills / Judith A. Tindall. -- 3rd ed.
     p. cm.
  ISBN 978-0-415-96233-9 (pbk. : alk. paper)
  1. Peer counseling--Problems, exercises, etc. I. Title.

BF637.C6T562 2008
158'.3--dc22   2008023487

Visit the Taylor & Francis Web site at
http://www.taylorandfrancis.com

and the Routledge Web site at
http://www.routledge.com

Peer Power, Book Two is dedicated to professional leaders who have gone the extra mile and continued training peers to have an impact on others. The energy and time it takes to make successful programs come from peer helpers becoming resources to others, as opposed to just gaining new skills.

This is the professional leaders' guide that accompanies the student workbook: *Peer Power, Book Two, Workbook.* This book is designed to provide you with the guidelines you need as a peer program professional to teach others advanced application skills in groups, tutoring, health and safety issues, leadership, and self-awareness. The decision was made to offer this as a separate book because often trainers still need their own training guide. If you need help with ideas for implementation of your program, please refer to *Peer Programs: An In-Depth Look at Peer Programs—Planning, Implementing and Administration, 2nd Edition.*

TABLE OF CONTENTS

INTRODUCTION .... **xiii**

**MODULE XIV   DRUG AND ALCOHOL ABUSE:
PREVENTION AND INTERVENTION** **1**

   Exercise 14.1 CHECKING MY KNOWLEDGE OF DRUGS
                       AND ALCOHOL 4
   Exercise 14.2 STAGES OF ADOLESCENT CHEMICAL USE 5
   Exercise 14.3 MY OWN CHEMICAL USE 6
   Exercise 14.4 TWENTY THINGS I LOVE TO DO AND MEANINGFUL
                       RELATIONSHIPS 7
   Exercise 14.5 PERSONAL INVENTORY 10
   Exercise 14.6 RECOGNIZING PROBLEMS IN OTHERS 11
   Exercise 14.7 PUTTING CONFRONTATION INTO ACTION 12
   Exercise 14.8 FAMILIES AFFECTED BY ALCOHOLISM 13
   Exercise 14.9 JUST SAY NO 14

**MODULE XV   TAKING CARE OF YOU!
STRESS MANAGEMENT** **17**

   Exercise 15.1 WHAT HAPPENS UNDER STRESS? 20
   Exercise 15.2 EFFECTS OF STRESS ON ME 21
   Exercise 15.3 HOW VULNERABLE ARE YOU TO STRESS? 22
   Exercise 15.4 COPING WITH STRESSORS 22
   Exercise 15.5 UNDERSTANDING THE DIFFERENCE BETWEEN
                       TENSION AND RELAXATION THROUGH IMAGERY 23
   Exercise 15.6 DEEP BREATHING 26
   Exercise 15.7 STRATEGIES FOR COPING WITH STRESS 27
   Exercise 15.8 BALANCED, HEALTHY LIFE 27
   Exercise 15.9 HEALTH HABITS AS A MEANS OF REDUCING
                       STRESS 29
   Exercise 15.10 THOUGHTS, FEELINGS, BEHAVIOR 30
   Exercise 15.11 EXAMINING YOUR SUPPORT SYSTEM 31
   Exercise 15.12 HOW TO BEAT STRESS 33
   Exercise 15.13 LONG-RANGE GOALS 35

**MODULE XVI   MENTAL HEALTH AWARENESS
AND REFERRAL** **37**

   Exercise 16.1 RECOGNIZING COMMON MENTAL HEALTH ISSUES ... 39
   Exercise 16.2 HOW TO RECOGNIZE OTHERS WITH MENTAL
                       HEALTH ISSUES 40
   Exercise 16.3 HOW TO REFER OTHERS WITH MENTAL HEALTH
                       ISSUES 41
   Exercise 16.4 HOW TO RAISE AWARENESS CONCERNING
                       MENTAL HEALTH 42

MODULE XVII LEADERSHIP TRAINING 43

Exercise 17.1 LEADERSHIP STYLE PROFILE 45
Exercise 17.2 LEADING A DISCUSSION GROUP 46
Exercise 17.3 WORKING WITH OTHERS 47
Exercise 17.4 TIME MANAGEMENT 48
Exercise 17.5 DEVELOPING AN ACTION PLAN 49
Exercise 17.6 PLANNING PUBLIC RELATIONS 50
Exercise 17.7 PLANNING A CONFERENCE OR OTHER MEETINGS. . . . 51
Exercise 17.8 BE A PURPOSE-DRIVEN LEADER 52

MODULE XVIII PEER HELPING THROUGH TUTORING 55

Exercise 18.1 SELF-ASSESSMENT 58
Exercise 18.2 HOW I STUDY 59
Exercise 18.3 HOW I LEARN BEST 60
Exercise 18.4 MAJOR STUDY SKILLS 62
Exercise 18.5 UNDERSTANDING MISBEHAVIOR OF OTHERS 63
Exercise 18.6 USING POSITIVE REINFORCERS FOR BEHAVIOR
               MANAGEMENT OF STUDENTS 63
Exercise 18.7 WILLIAM GLASSER: HOW TO DISCIPLINE 64
Exercise 18.8 PROBLEMS IN TUTORING 65
Exercise 18.9 PUTTING TUTORING SKILLS INTO ACTION. 66

MODULE XIX PEER HELPING THROUGH GROUP WORK: PEER EDUCATION AND SUPPORT 69

Exercise 19.1   SELF-ASSESSMENT OF GROUP FACILITATOR
                SKILLS...................................... 72
Exercise 19.2   FUNCTIONS OF A DISCUSSION FACILITATOR 73
Exercise 19.3   LEADING A DISCUSSION GROUP 74
Exercise 19.4   LIFE PROBLEMS GROUP......................... 75
Exercise 19.5   SUBJECT MATTER GROUP 75
Exercise 19.6   DECISION-MAKING GROUP....................... 76
Exercise 19.7   CHECKLIST OF SKILLS FOR CLASSROOM GROUP 77
Exercise 19.8   UNDERSTANDING OTHERS 78
Exercise 19.9   MOTIVATING OTHERS........................... 79
Exercise 19.10 PUBLIC SPEAKING SKILLS 80
Exercise 19.11 PLANNING FOR LARGE GROUPS 81
Exercise 19.12 PRACTICE A LARGE CLASSROOM GROUP
                PRESENTATION................................ 82

MODULE XX ENHANCING SEXUAL HEALTH THROUGH PEER HELPING.. 85

Exercise 20.1 HOW MUCH DO YOU KNOW ABOUT HIV/AIDS AND
               STDs? 87
Exercise 20.2 HIV/AIDS..................................... 90
Exercise 20.3 STDs 91

Exercise 20.4	LEARNING THE LANGUAGE OF STDs, HIV, AND AIDS.	92
Exercise 20.5	REDUCING RISKY BEHAVIOR THROUGH SEXUAL RESPONSIBILITY.	92
Exercise 20.6	DECISION MAKING	93

MODULE XXI RECOGNIZING DISORDERED EATING PROBLEMS 95

Exercise 21.1	FOOD CHART	98
Exercise 21.2	ASSESSING DISORDERED EATING	99
Exercise 21.3	BULIMIA, ANOREXIA, COMPULSIVE OVEREATING: WHERE ARE YOU AS A DISORDERED EATING PERSON OR ENABLER?	100
Exercise 21.4	FOOD CHOICE EVALUATION	101
Exercise 21.5	CULTURAL IMPACT OF DISORDERED EATING.	101
Exercise 21.6	BODY IMAGE AND THE IMPACT ON DISORDERED EATING	103
Exercise 21.7	PRACTICE IN HELPING A PERSON WITH DISORDERED EATING.	103
Exercise 21.8	LOOKING AT MYSELF.	104

MODULE XXII SUICIDE PREVENTION 107

Exercise 22.1	STRESS SELF-EVALUATION	109
Exercise 22.2	SUICIDE RISKS	110
Exercise 22.3	INTERVENTION TECHNIQUES	111
Exercise 22.4	ASSISTING THOSE LEFT TO LIVE ON AFTER A SUICIDE.	112
Exercise 22.5	PRACTICE IN HELPING A SUICIDAL PERSON.	113

MODULE XXIII COPING WITH LOSS 115

Exercise 23.1	MY OWN LOSSES	117
Exercise 23.2	TYPES OF LOSS.	117
Exercise 23.3	THE GRIEVING PROCESS	118
Exercise 23.4	OFFERING SUPPORT TO OTHERS	119

MODULE XXIV HIGHWAY TRAFFIC SAFETY 121

Exercise 24.1	THE FACTS OF HIGHWAY TRAFFIC SAFETY	123
Exercise 24.2	YOUTH RISK FACTORS: HIGHWAY TRAFFIC SAFETY	124
Exercise 24.3	COUNTERMEASURES FOR HIGHWAY TRAFFIC SAFETY	124
Exercise 24.4	SOCIAL NORMS APPROACH	125
Exercise 24.5	STRATEGIES FOR IMPACTING OTHERS TO DRIVE SAFELY	126

MODULE XXV BULLYING REDUCTION 129
Exercise 25.1 WHAT IS BULLYING? 133
Exercise 25.2 EFFECTS OF BULLYING ON ME 134
Exercise 25.3 HELPING OTHERS WITH BULLYING............... 135

MODULE XXVI PEER HELPING THROUGH MENTORING 139
Exercise 26.1 MY MENTOR 141
Exercise 26.2 MY PEER HELPING ROLE AS A MENTOR 142
Exercise 26.3 DEVELOPING A RELATIONSHIP WITH MY MENTEE... 143
Exercise 26.4 HOW DID THINGS GO? 144
Exercise 26.5 MENTORING REFLECTIONS 145

MODULE XXVII A PEER HELPER'S ROLE IN CRISIS MANAGEMENT 147
Exercise 27.1 WHAT IS A POTENTIALLY TRAUMATIZING EVENT?... 149
Exercise 27.2 RECOGNIZING SIGNS OF POSTTRAUMATIC STRESS DISORDER (PTSD) AND STRESS DISORDER. 150
Exercise 27.3 DEFINITIONS................................. 151
Exercise 27.4 CRITICAL ISSUES IN PEER HELPING PROVIDING CRISIS MANAGEMENT 152

MODULE XXVIII PEER HELPING THROUGH CHARACTER EDUCATION DEVELOPMENT 155
Exercise 28.1 STEPS FOR A CHARACTER EDUCATION TRAINING SESSION 159
Exercise 28.2 RESPONSIBILITY.............................. 160
Exercise 28.3 SERVICE (CITIZENSHIP) 161
Exercise 28.4 HONESTY, RESPONSIBILITY..................... 162
Exercise 28.5 HUMANITY, RESPECT 163
Exercise 28.6 HONESTY, SELF-ESTEEM 163
Exercise 28.7 HONESTY, RESPECT, PERSEVERANCE, AND GOAL-SETTING 164

MODULE XXIX PROBLEM GAMBLING: PREVENTION AND INTERVENTION 167
Exercise 29.1 WHAT ARE TYPES OF GAMBLING? 171
Exercise 29.2 PROBLEM GAMBLING SELF-TEST FOR TEENS 172
Exercise 29.3 PRACTICE HELPING OTHERS WITH GAMBLING ISSUES 173

MODULE XXX YOUTH TOBACCO PREVENTION THROUGH COMMUNITY IMPACT 175
Exercise 30.1 TOBACCO ISSUES.............................. 177
Exercise 30.2 TOBACCO MARKETS TO YOUTH 178

Exercise 30.3 IMPACTING THE COMMUNITY: PREVENTION OF
               TOBACCO USE OF YOUTH 179
Exercise 30.4 STRATEGIES TO HELP YOUTH STAY
               TOBACCO-FREE 180

ADDITIONAL RESOURCES **183**

AUTHOR **185**

NOTE: Modules I through XIII are in *Peer Power, Book One* and in *Peer Power, Book One, Workbook.*

INTRODUCTION

Peer Power, Book Two is designed to assist your peer helpers to grow interpersonally, gain new skills, and have the tools to work with others. The modules can be taught separately, depending on the focus of the program and the issues that your program wants to address.

Before you begin *Peer Power, Book Two*, it is important to review the *Peer Programs* book to review training skills and utilization of peer programs and evaluation chapters. The whole book is helpful in planning activities for your peer helper group. The activities and advanced training are guided by peer helper development, the helpers taking care of themselves, and delivery of issues relevant to the population they serve.

The manner in which you (the peer program professional) decide how to utilize the following skills is up to you. The most important aspect of the peer-led strategy is that peer helpers have an opportunity to utilize their skills with others. Just learning these application exercises is not enough. Peer helpers must help others through one-on-one helping or group education and support, and then have an opportunity to reflect on what they have completed.

The 17 modules (XIV through XXX) may be taken in any order. Each is independent.

Module XIV: Drug and Alcohol Abuse will help the peer helpers understand their own drug and alcohol use, as well as recognize the problem in others. Intervention skills will also be learned.

Module XV: Taking Care of You! Stress Management is essential to help the peer helpers stay healthy and manage their own stress as they try to help others. This is designed to assist the peer helpers assess their current way of living and design a behavior change program to help create a healthier lifestyle. Peer helpers can then utilize the information learned to help others individually or in groups.

Module XVI: Mental Health Awareness and Referral is designed to assist the peer helper in becoming a more fully functioning individual. First, it is important to recognize common mental health issues in yourself and others. Learning tools to manage mental health, and make referrals if needed, is helpful. Peer helpers serve as models for others and help to take the stigma out of seeking professional help for mental health issues.

As peer helpers become more skilled in communicating with others, either individually or in groups, it is important for them to develop specific leadership skills. As the trainees complete Module XVII: Leadership Training, peer helpers will examine their current leadership styles and techniques to effectively serve others.

One important step is the skill of tutoring others. Module XVIII: Peer Helping Through Tutoring will guide the peer helper through necessary steps to become an effective tutor.

If you decide to utilize peer helpers in a group setting, they will need specific skills. Module XIX: Peer Helping Through Group Work: Peer Education and Support will assist the peer helper in leading small and large groups to educate others. Peer helpers can present peer education from various modules in this book, including wellness, eating disorders, drug and alcohol awareness, coping with loss, suicide prevention, highway traffic safety, and others.

Peer helpers are a powerful influence in saving lives and can help reduce health concerns related to sexual issues. Human sexual health peer facilitators can be effective in reaching target populations that do not respond to traditional education. Peers can be used to educate, facilitate referrals, and counsel. Module XX: Enhancing Sexual Health Through Peer Helping will assist peer helpers in helping others with sexual health issues.

At times, peer helpers need help in recognizing eating problems they may have, as well as how to recognize an eating disorder in others. Module XXI: Recognizing Disordered

Eating Problems will assist peer helpers in learning about anorexia, bulimia, and compulsive overeating.

Peer helpers also need to have skills in recognizing suicidal signs in others, and know how to refer those needing professional help. Module XXII: Suicide Prevention will assist in this skill.

Peer helpers can be effective in helping peers through the grief process. Module XXIII: Coping with Loss will assist you in helping those in need.

Module XXIV: Highway Traffic Safety is a critical issue facing people today. These safety practices can save lives and need to be delivered by peers in a variety of ways. This module will provide information about the issue and suggest some follow-up strategies.

As peer helpers, it is important to recognize bullying behavior in others. Bullying can have an impact on the victim, as well as the bully. Lessons concerning how to recognize this behavior and strategies for helping will be developed in Module XXV: Bullying Reduction. Bullying lessons are effective in the workplace, as well as in schools. Bullying education can be a part of an overall approach to violence prevention that includes peer mediation programs and peer listening programs.

Peer mentors have been helpful with students who are new to a school, organization, or are at-risk for failure. Module XXVI: Peer Helping Through Mentoring will give you another approach that can help in providing assistance to others. Basic communication skills learned in *Peer Power, Book One* are necessary to be effective in this role.

Module XXVII: A Peer Helper's Role in Crisis Management is helpful to those who want to be a part of helping others through a crisis. Most organizations have a crisis plan in place. Peer helpers can assist with the plan by listening to others, recognizing impairment in others, and having professional referral skills.

Building good citizenship and character with youth is essential to the development of a caring society. Module XXVIII: Peer Helping Through Character Education Development will set a plan in place to deliver character education to younger youth, as well as to serve as a positive role model.

Gambling addiction can be devastating, whether it's sports betting, horse racing, casinos, cards, or other games. If peer helpers can recognize gambling addiction in others, they should use intervention and referral skills. Educating others to the dangers of gambling addiction will be developed in Module XXIX: Problem Gambling: Prevention and Intervention.

Peer helpers can have an impact on their community by advocating for a safer, healthier environment. Lessons covering smoking and strategies that discourage students from smoking will be presented in Module XXX: Youth Tobacco Prevention Through Community Impact.

Peer helpers may want to evaluate their own skills through the self-evaluation. This could be a pre- and postassessment.

My hope is that you will utilize these exercises to meet your own curriculum design. You may use some or all of the exercises, depending on the development needed by your peer helpers and the focus of your program.

It is important that peer helpers have a foundation in the basic skills that can be found in *Peer Power, Book One, Workbook*.

TRAINING MODULE TIMELINES

An approximation of the amount of time that needs to be allotted for each module has been included to facilitate scheduling requirements for the entire training program. Modifications can be made to facilitate the maximum growth of trainees with whom one is working. However, with the first group of trainees, the recommendation is that one adheres fairly closely to the suggested time schedule. Table 1.1 is an outline of the time schedule for Modules XIV through XXX.

TABLE I.1 APPROXIMATE TIME SCHEDULE SUGGESTED FOR EACH TRAINING SESSION AND FOR APPLICATION TIMES FOR EACH MODULE

Module	Topic	Time – exercise	Time	Age group
XIV	Drug and Alcohol Abuse: Prevention and Intervention	435–750	395	H.S.–adult
XXV	Taking Care of You! Stress Management	640	470	H.S.–adult
XXVI	Mental Health Awareness and Referral	210–330	120	H.S.–adult
XVII	Leadership Training	450–570	240	H.S.–adult
XVIII	Peer Helping Through Tutoring	390–760	445	M.S.–adult
XIX	Peer Helping Through Group Work: Peer Education and Support	870–1360	335	H.S.–adult
XX	Enhancing Sexual Health Through Peer Helping	240–400	85	H.S.–adult
XXI	Recognizing Disordered Eating	390–590	220	H.S.–adult
XXII	Suicide Prevention	240–370	120	H.S.–adult
XXIII	Coping with Loss	240–270	130	H.S.–adult
XXIV	Highway Traffic Safety	210–360	235	H.S.–adult
XXV	Bullying Reduction	90–180	85	M.S.–adult
XXVI	Peer Helping Through Mentoring	175–300	120	Upper elementary–adult
XXVII	A Peer Helper's Role in Crisis Management	125–270	80	H.S.–adult
XXVIII	Peer Helping Through Character Education Development	300–510	180	M.S.–adult
XXIX	Problem Gambling: Prevention and Intervention	90–180	75	H.S.–adult
XXX	Youth Tobacco Prevention Through Community Impact	90–180	60	H.S.–adult
	Total for Book Two			
	In minutes	4,954–8,020	3,395	
	In hours	82–134	57	

Introduction xvii

The time is further subdivided by exercise, which can be taught individually or combined, where needed.

The total time requirement will depend upon several factors, such as ability and/or prior experience of trainees, time blocked for each training session, and opportunity for practice and preparation between training sessions. Because training conditions will vary from location to location, the training program is organized into modules with subdivisions (exercises) that can be taught individually or combined to meet local circumstances.

The overall approximate time allowance for modules is provided in the previous table. For planning the training program, times can be used as guides. When exercises are grouped together to be taught in the same module, the total time span usually will be less than when each exercise is taught separately.

PHYSICAL ARRANGEMENT AND EQUIPMENT

The physical arrangements for a peer helping training program can be very simple or elaborate. The room must be large enough for practicing the various roles. Movable chairs are important. Acoustics are important because of the interaction desired among trainees during the training sessions.

A whiteboard or flip chart will assist in the training. Some of the information sections can easily be put in PowerPoint. A means of writing notes large enough for viewing by all trainees is also important.

Video and audio equipment for recording and playback are helpful for reinforcement and mobility. Trainees often are able to benefit from video viewing of previously prepared recordings of skills being taught and of themselves during practice.

Each trainee will need to have a copy of *Peer Power, Book Two, Workbook*, and the leader will need a copy of *Peer Power, Book Two*.

NUMBER AND AGE OF TRAINEES

The number of trainees in any given program is limited by the number of trainers, persons (potential trainees) available, facilities, and the need for peer helpers once the training program is completed. A minimum number at one time to facilitate the interaction suggested in many of the exercises is three. The maximum number, with one peer helping professional, would be 12 to 16, with 9 to 12 being a more ideal number. If you have larger training groups, it is important to have other professionals available to assist the small training groups. For example, if you have a space large enough for 60 participants, you will need one professional for each 12 trainees. One main facilitator can coordinate the training. The age span is upper elementary students through adult.

FORMAT OF TRAINING SUGGESTIONS

Each module and exercise has purposes, introductory information, training procedures in sequential order, and homework assignments for trainees between training sessions. The trainer may want to record some of the training to assist trainees.

MODULE

DRUG AND ALCOHOL ABUSE: PREVENTION AND INTERVENTION

Goals

To introduce trainees to introductory material concerning drug and alcohol abuse

To raise awareness of their own chemical use

To look at alternative ways for coping with life

Approximate Time

Module Introduction

Application—10 to 15 minutes

Exercise 14.1—60 to 120 minutes in training session
Application—60 to 120 minutes

Exercise 14.2—30 to 60 minutes in training session
Application—20 minutes

Exercise 14.3—60 to 120 minutes in training session
Application—60 minutes

Exercise 14.4—60 to 120 minutes in training session

Exercise 14.5—15 to 30 minutes in training session
Application—60 minutes

Exercise 14.6—30 to 60 minutes in training session
Application—15 minutes

Exercise 14.7—60 to 120 minutes in training session

Exercise 14.8—60 to 120 minutes in training session
Application—30 minutes

Exercise 14.9—60 minutes in training session
Application—15 minutes

Materials

- *Peer Power, Book Two, Workbook* (one copy for each trainee)
- Optional: Video equipment with video of the confrontation and intervention
- Speaker on alcohol and substance abuse from the local community

Introduction to the Module

Drug and alcohol abuse is one of the major problems facing Americans today. In part, it is a problem because many individuals lack awareness of how chemicals affect their minds and bodies and thus have a difficult time learning how to lead a healthy, happy life free of chemicals. Suggest activities and relationships that will be helpful, and train the peer counselors in the use of confrontation when an intervention is necessary for a friend or family member.

You may want to supplement this module with speakers and films concerning drugs and alcohol. They also may want to use the form in Exercise SD4.3, *Peer Power, Book One*, for setting goals.

Training Procedures

1. Decide number of training sessions and exercises to be included in each session.
2. Review content to be covered and suggested activities as listed in *Peer Power, Book Two, Workbook*.
3. Be prepared to do a demonstration of confrontation, or have videos of behaviors to be taught.
4. If a speaker or film is used, you may want to schedule it in the early part of training. The National Council on Alcoholism and Drug Dependence has excellent films at reasonable cost.
5. You may want trainees to do research on the impact of drugs on the brain through the Internet. There are several suggested resources.
6. Refer to the *Peer Programs* book to learn about the rationale for peer programs to reduce drugs and alcohol. Use J.10 on reflection from the CD of the *Peer Programs* book.

Evaluation Process

As a trainer, you can evaluate the process used in teaching a skill by the feedback obtained from trainees, by observations of their written work, and by their behavior when practicing the skill during training sessions.

Measuring Outcomes

1. Use Exercise 14.1 concerning the review quiz and puzzle and Exercises 14.2 and 14.3 to identify the effects of chemicals and the awareness of their use.
2. Use Exercises 14.4 and 14.5 to examine the process and awareness of alternative approaches to drugs and alcohol.
3. Watch and listen closely during the practice in Exercise 14.7 to measure the ease with which trainees are using confrontation in terms of intervention.

EXERCISE 14.1
CHECKING MY KNOWLEDGE OF
DRUGS AND ALCOHOL

Goal

To learn some of the symptoms of alcoholism and drug abuse in order to become aware of the problems they cause

Introduction to the Module

In Exercise 14.1 the trainees will learn about the effects of alcohol and drug abuse and the impact it has on the brain. They will learn to identify how serious the chemical problem is with someone they know. This exercise is designed to make trainees aware of these problems.

Training Procedures

1. Discuss the material presented concerning drugs and alcohol with trainees.

2. The trainer may want to show a film or ask a speaker to talk to the group concerning the effects of chemicals.

3. "Twenty-Six Questions" is excellent to assess the trainees' personal use or friends' use of alcohol.

4. Review the information on common signs of drug use and the impact on the brain.

5. Ask trainees to complete the "Drug and Alcohol Review Quiz" and to review the "Common Signs of Other Drug Use."

6. The trainees may have a hard time believing the effects of drugs and alcohol and may even challenge the trainer concerning the problem. The purpose is not to get into a debate, but to encourage them to do further reading about the problem.

7. Assign Exercise 14.1 sheets for homework.

Application for Trainees After the Group Meeting

1. Ask trainees to complete Exercise 14.1 by the next meeting.
2. Prepare for Exercise 14.2.

EXERCISE 14.2
STAGES OF ADOLESCENT CHEMICAL USE

Goals

To review how chemical abuse happens in stages

To help adolescents examine their own use, as well as that of others

Introduction to the Exercise

In Exercise 14.1, the trainees learned about the effect of chemicals. In Exercise 14.2, the trainees will learn about their own and others' chemical use and how it affects them.

Training Procedures

1. Review the material from Exercise 14.1.
2. Discuss the material in Exercise 14.2 in terms of whether or not the trainees agree with it.
3. Emphasize trust, which is very important in proceeding with this exercise.
4. Ask the trainees to identify people they know who struggle with chemical use and abuse, and in what stage they are.
5. Ask the trainees to examine the different stages of chemical use and decide which stage of chemical abuse they are in. If any of the trainees bring up their own problems, they may need to be referred to outside help.
6. Ask them what they have learned from the activity.
7. Ask the trainees to turn in their homework from Exercise 14.1.

Application for Trainees After the Group Meeting

Ask trainees to prepare for Exercise 14.3.

EXERCISE 14.3
MY OWN CHEMICAL USE

Goal

To provide trainees an opportunity to assess their own chemical use

Introduction to the Exercise

In Exercise 14.1, trainees learned about the effect of chemicals. In Exercise 14.2, they learned the stages of adolescent chemical use. In Exercise 14.3, trainees will learn about their own use of chemicals, and how it affects them.

Training Procedures

1. Review the material from Exercises 14.1 and 14.2, as well as information from the speaker and other research.
2. Discuss the material in terms of whether or not trainees agree with it.
3. Ask trainees to identify others they know who have had a chemical problem.
4. Ask trainees to turn in homework from Exercise 14.2.
5. Ask trainees to examine their own chemical use. Use the exercise as a guide for discussion.
6. Ask trainees what they have learned from the activity.
7. This exercise will be helpful if the training group trusts each other. They should have developed trust by this time.
8. Some trainees may have a problem with chemicals. Suggest that they seek outside professional help.
9. Have the trainees set goals concerning their use and how they would like to change their life this week.

Application for Trainees After the Group Meeting

Ask trainees to work on their goal concerning chemicals for the week.

EXERCISE 14.4
TWENTY THINGS I LOVE TO DO AND MEANINGFUL RELATIONSHIPS

Goal

To provide an opportunity for trainees to examine their activities and relationships and to see if they are leading a healthy, fulfilling life

Introduction to the Exercise

As individuals begin to turn away from drugs and alcohol abuse and look at a healthier lifestyle, or as they begin to look at ways to prevent abuse, it is important to examine the kinds of activities they love and the types of relationships they have.

This exercise can be used in two ways: to see if the activities and relationships are helping trainees lead a chemical-free life and to change the activities and relationships if they represent an unhealthy lifestyle. It is important to examine these areas first.

Training Procedures

1. Refer to "Twenty Things I Love to Do." Encourage trainees to start filling out their lists by suggesting, "They can be big things or little things." Offer an example or two, or suggest, "You might think in terms of the seasons of the year for things you love to do." As the trainer, draw up your own list of 20 items. Explain to trainees that it is all right if they have more or less than 20 items on their lists.
2. When the lists are done, tell the students to use the rows of boxes on their papers to code their lists in the following manner.

a. A dollar sign ($) is to be placed beside any item that costs more than $5 each time it is done.

b. The letter A is to be placed beside those items the trainee really prefers to do alone.

The letter P is placed next to activities that the trainee prefers to do with other people.

The letters AP should be placed next to activities that the trainee enjoys doing alone or with other people.

c. The letters PL are to be placed beside those that require planning.

d. The code N5 is to be placed next to those items that would not have been listed 5 years ago.

e. The numbers 1 through 5 are to be placed beside the five most important items. The best-loved activity should be number 1, the second best 2, and so on.

f. The trainee is to indicate next to each activity when it was last engaged in (day and date).

g. Place a CHEM beside any activity that includes chemicals.

h. Use the following additional suggestions for coding:

R—Those things on the list that have an element of *risk* to them (physical, emotional, or intellectual risk).

I—Any item that involves *intimacy*.

S—Any item that can be done only in a particular *season* of the year.

Q—Any item that you think you would enjoy more if you were *smarter*.

U—Any item that you think others would judge as *unconventional*.

C—Any item that you think others would judge as *conventional*.

MT—Any item that you think you will want to devote increasingly *more time* to in years to come.

CH—Any item that you hope your own *children* will have on their lists someday.

RE—Any item that no one would *reject* you for doing because you love to do it.

3. Discuss with the trainees their results.
   - Do they see a pattern?
   - Ask under what circumstance they like to engage in a chosen activity.
   - Ask the trainees to look at the items listed in Direction 1. Think of advantages, pleasures, gains, benefits, or satisfaction they gain from the activity.
4. Ask them if the activities are chemical-free or if this is part of their lives.
5. If desired, give the trainees this activity again after the end of training to see if responses are different.
6. Have trainees look at "Assessment of Meaningful Relationships" and select 10 friends who are most significant to them today. Assess each friend selected according to the requirements of the worksheet.
7. Discuss results.
   - Did they discover anything about themselves?
   - Were they surprised?
   - Were they disappointed in what they uncovered?
   - How many of the relationships involve spending time with chemicals?
8. Ask trainees to think about their activities and relationships, and to set any goals to make changes in either.

Application for Trainees After the Group Meeting

Ask trainees to work on goals for different activities and relationships.

EXERCISE 14.5
PERSONAL INVENTORY

Goals

To help trainees consider alternative highs for activities

To help trainees think of alternative highs for any group they belong to

Introduction to the Exercise

1. Ask trainees how they are doing with their goals from Exercises 14.2, 14.3, and 14.4, and ask them to set future goals (30 minutes).
2. Ask trainees to list ways they get high other than from chemicals. There is a list suggested, but assist them in coming up with other ways. Ask them to explain these in written form.
3. Ask students to circle any of the stereotypes they fit into and ask if they would like to change.
4. Help students explore ways in which the group they belong to can find an alternative high.
5. Help trainees set goals concerning alternative highs and changing stereotypes.

Application for Trainees After the Group Meeting

Ask trainees to continue working on goals for Exercise 14.4 and to begin working on goals for Exercise 14.5. Examples of alternative highs might be to learn to play tennis, go jogging, plan a dance for the school, ask a good friend to go to a movie, or prepare a gourmet meal.

EXERCISE 14.6
RECOGNIZING PROBLEMS IN OTHERS

Goal

To help trainees examine others' behavior in terms of their chemical use, and how this affects them and what they would like to have done (helpful when trying to engage in a confrontation)

Introduction to the Exercise

Peer helpers are often called on to help when someone wants to confront another person with their chemical use. The following exercise will help the trainee keep a journal.

Training Procedures

1. Discuss the reaction to Exercise 14.5.
2. Have the trainees write examples of what has happened when a family member or friend abused chemicals.
3. Have the trainees write the date and behavior, then the feeling, reaction, and what behavior would be better in the future.

   Example:

   (6/25) Drank so much I passed out at party—angry/frustrated—cried—I'm not to drink at parties.

4. From the chart, have them create a plan of confrontation.

Guidelines for Confrontation

1. Confrontation is an individualized plan of action.
2. Confrontation must be done out of love, not malice, resentment, or retaliation.

   a. Abuser must be confronted when not under the influence and at an appropriate time and place.

   b. A genuine statement must be sent: "I feel _____."

c. Circumstances must be stated simply.

   d. Discussion and actions must be calm and caring.

3. Before confrontation is made, you must develop:

   a. A sense of direction

   b. A sense of confidence

   c. A sense of well-being

Application for Trainees After the Group Meeting

Ask trainees to continue with the chart and plan.

EXERCISE 14.7
PUTTING CONFRONTATION INTO ACTION

Goal

To help trainees use their skills in confrontation, assertiveness, and genuineness in an intervention activity

Introduction to the Exercise

Peer helpers often become aware that someone is having a chemical problem. It is frustrating not knowing what to do about the problem. Sometimes it is good to work with a professional counselor to help facilitate the confrontation concerning drugs and alcohol. This activity also can be used with a friend or family member.

Training Procedures

1. Discuss intervention and its purpose. Suggest the option of having a professional counselor present.

2. Ask trainees to divide into groups of three.

3. Ask the group members to choose one of the situations given or one with which they are familiar.

4. Have each trainee play one of three roles: the confronter, the person with the problem, and the facilitator.

5. Rotate around the groups to discuss the activity.

6. As trainer, role-play one of the situations.

7. Encourage trainees to use all the skills they have learned thus far.

8. Discuss the experience.

Application for Trainees After the Group Meeting

Ask trainees to continue to work on their own personal goals and read introduction to Exercise 14.8.

EXERCISE 14.8
FAMILIES AFFECTED BY ALCOHOLISM

Goal

To focus on the effect alcohol has on the family

Introduction to the Exercise

Alcoholism not only affects the alcoholic, but it also affects the alcoholic's family. An important aspect of this exercise is to assist trainees in identifying symptoms and finding some help for the dysfunctional family.

Training Procedures

1. Discuss the intervention and the purpose of the intervention from Exercise 14.7.

2. If possible, obtain a film or video about adult children of alcoholics, or one that shows addiction is a family affair.

3. Ask the trainees to read the material from this exercise and discuss each point.

4. Ask the trainees if they identify with some of the roles in the family of an alcoholic.

5. Focus on the differences in the bodily reaction of a social drinker versus that of an alcoholic drinker.

6. Help the trainees focus on their own family in terms of possible alcoholism.

7. Help the trainees focus on others by having them role-play, with one person being the child of an alcoholic and another playing the helper and using the information available.

8. Refer them to the appropriate outside help.

9. Have the peer helpers do research on the Internet or write for information.

Application for Trainees After the Group Meeting

Have the trainees write their reaction to the activities.

EXERCISE 14.9
JUST SAY NO

Goal

To help the trainees practice saying no to peer pressure

Introduction to the Exercise

Peer helpers are role models for others in terms of leading a healthy lifestyle. This exercise is to be used by the training group; at other times it could be used in groups that the peer counselor facilitates or in a classroom presentation.

The trainees need to be encouraged to identify levels of alcohol use in themselves and others and to identify peer pressure to use alcohol in social or party settings. The trainees need to realize that the danger of alcohol lies in the relative ease in obtaining it and its social acceptability over other drugs. The trainees need to see the positive consequences of nonuse or use in moderation (as an adult) and the negative consequences of misuse, abuse, and dependence. The trainees should be asked to define the difference between use and abuse of alcohol and to express ways of avoiding peer pressure to misuse alcohol.

Training Procedures

1. Discuss peer pressure and its meaning.
2. Discuss the terms *nonuse, use, abuse,* and *dependence.* Ask for examples of each.
3. Discuss the concept of peer pressure. Ask for definitions and/or examples. Peer pressure has no age limit. Give examples of peer pressure in the young and old, as well as outcomes such as vandalizing or buying a certain car.
4. Discuss how easily students are exposed to alcohol by asking them about their personal introduction to it. Be sure to emphasize the party setting. Discuss parties and what these mean.
5. Discuss how some individuals misuse alcohol at parties. Give examples.
6. Ask the members to discuss the consequences of nonuse and abuse.
7. Ask the trainees how they can put a limit on their use.
8. Divide the group into triads. Ask them to practice playing roles at a party where everyone is drinking. One person decides to say no. Change roles so that all of the members have a chance to play each role.
9. Lead a discussion on consequences.

Application for Trainees After the Group Meeting

1. Have trainees write in their journal how it felt to say no.
2. Use J.10 about reflection for evaluation from the *Peer Programs* book CD.

MODULE XV

TAKING CARE OF YOU! STRESS MANAGEMENT

Goals

To help trainees become aware of their own stressors

To help trainees learn effective techniques for coping with stress

To help trainees move toward a lifestyle of wellness that will provide them with tools to take care of themselves

Approximate Time

Module Introduction

Application—60 minutes

Exercise 15.1—60 minutes in training session

Application—60 minutes

Exercise 15.2—60 minutes in training session

Application—60 minutes

Exercise 15.3—40 minutes in training session

Application—15 minutes

Exercise 15.4—60 minutes in training session

Application—60 minutes

Exercise 15.5—60 minutes in training session
Application—30 minutes

Exercise 15.6—15 minutes in training session
Application—30 minutes

Exercise 15.7—30 minutes in training session
Application—30 minutes

Exercise 15.8—60 minutes in training session
Application—30 minutes

Exercise 15.9—60 minutes in training session
Application—20 minutes

Exercise 15.10—60 minutes in training session
Application—60 minutes

Exercise 15.11—60 minutes in training session
Application—15 minutes

Exercise 15.12—30 minutes in training session
Application—15 minutes

Exercise 15.13—30 minutes in training session
Application—15 minutes

Materials

- *Peer Power, Book Two, Workbook* (one copy for each trainee)
- Whiteboard or flip pad and pen
- Optional: Tapes for relaxation

Introduction to the Module

In this module, trainees will have an opportunity to learn about how to take care of themselves and the effective management of stress. The peer program professional may want to use the goal-setting materials described in *Peer Power, Book One, Workbook* to assist in changing behavior. It is important for leaders to model the kinds of responses they want the trainees to use. The techniques taught in this module naturally follow the drug and alcohol module because it assists trainees in moving toward a healthier lifestyle and managing stress. This module is simply an introduction to stress management and self-care. For changes to be permanent, we would suggest working with a group for a minimum of 12 meetings on changing lifestyles (this could be in weight loss, smoking cessation, exercise, etc.). The most important thing is to help trainees become aware of how they need to make some changes in their lifestyle.

Training Procedures

1. Select exercises for the training sessions. Each selection will make a difference in homework assignments and the time available for each exercise.

2. Follow the sequence of exercises and the training procedures for each.

3. Arrange for DVDs, if desired, for use.

4. Arrange for goal-setting sheets to be available to trainees.

5. Model each exercise with the trainer expressing their own stressors.

6. Use J.10 from the CD in *Peer Programs*.

Evaluation Process

Evaluate the process used in the teaching of the skill by the feedback obtained from trainees, by observations and written work, and from their behavior when they are asked to set goals.

Measuring Outcomes

1. Use Exercises 15.1, 15.2, and 15.3 to identify stressors, stress reaction, and effective techniques for coping with stressors.

2. Use Exercise 15.8 to look at setting goals for a balanced lifestyle. Use Exercise 15.13 for setting long-range goals.

EXERCISE 15.1
WHAT HAPPENS UNDER STRESS?

Goal

To help trainees understand stress, and to help them identify the events that cause stress in their lives

Introduction to the Exercise

This exercise is designed to help trainees learn about stress and discuss the issue of stress with their trainer. You may decide to show a DVD on stress management. The exercise is most beneficial to trainees, as it helps them identify stressors through the personal appraisal form.

Training Procedures

1. Review goals set from Module XIV and assess progress.
2. Review the introductory material to this module and for Exercise 15.1.
3. Show a DVD on stress and wellness, if available.
4. Discuss the area of stress and wellness and, for those who are interested, suggest some of the related books listed in the trainer's manual.
5. Ask trainees to fill out the personal appraisal form to help identify stressors.
6. Discuss the responses.

Example:

- When do you feel most stressed?
- Who do you feel most stressed around?
- What did you learn about yourself concerning your stressors?

Application for Trainees After the Group Meeting

1. Ask trainees to continue working on goals from Module XIV and setting new goals.
2. Have trainees identify stressors in your life during the next day (or week).
3. Assign Exercise 15.2, "Effects of Stress on Me."

EXERCISE 15.2
EFFECTS OF STRESS ON ME

Goal

To enable trainees to understand the effects of their own stress, both in a positive and negative manner

Introduction to the Exercise

This exercise is designed to convey to the trainees that stress can be both positive and negative and to assist the trainees in identifying how stress affects them.

Training Procedures

1. Review goals from Module XIV and assess progress.
2. Review stressors and discuss additional stressors identified by trainees.
3. Ask trainees to review positive and negative effects of stress.
4. Have trainees work with a partner to help identify effects of stress on them.
5. Discuss results.
6. Have trainees turn in Exercise 15.2 for trainer feedback.

Application for Trainees After the Group Meeting

1. Ask trainees to continue to work on goals from Module XIV.
2. Encourage trainees to begin identifying positive and negative effects of stress on trainee.

EXERCISE 15.3
HOW VULNERABLE ARE YOU TO STRESS?

Goal

To assist trainees in examining how vulnerable they are to stress

Introduction to the Exercise

It is important to understand the concept of vulnerability to stress and how to assess one's vulnerability.

Training Procedures

1. Review the background on vulnerability to stress. The peer program professional will need to explain areas that are not clear.
2. Have trainees complete the questionnaire.
3. Have trainees discuss how to take care of themselves to protect against stress.

Application for Trainees After the Group Meeting

Ask the trainees to work on one area of their lives to protect against stress.

EXERCISE 15.4
COPING WITH STRESSORS

Goal

To assist trainees in examining effective and ineffective techniques for coping with stressors

Introduction to the Exercise

Review Exercises 15.1 and 15.2 and return material handed in. This is a very important exercise and begins to help trainees learn new ways of coping with stress.

Training Procedures

1. List stressors and how they affect the trainee (reaction). The trainer models what is wanted by using the chalkboard.
2. Have trainees discuss stressors and their effects.
3. Ask trainees to work with a partner to develop how they can handle stress (both ineffectively and effectively).
4. The trainer asks the group to list effective and ineffective techniques for coping with stress. List methods on a chalkboard and have someone duplicate them for the group. This may assist group members in coming up with effective techniques.
5. Refer to goal-setting techniques from *Peer Power, Book One, Workbook*.
6. Ask trainees to try a new effective coping technique.

Application for Trainees After the Group Meeting

Ask trainees to work on a goal to effectively lower stress by handling the stressor differently.

EXERCISE 15.5
UNDERSTANDING THE DIFFERENCE BETWEEN TENSION AND RELAXATION THROUGH IMAGERY

Goal

To enable the trainees to know the difference between tension and relaxation

Introduction to the Exercise

This exercise uses imagery to help the trainees visualize tension and relaxation. Have the room as quiet as possible, with low lighting. The use of some quiet music in the background is also effective.

Training Procedures

1. Read the following script in a calm and even voice:

   Please get as comfortable as possible and close your eyes to better feel the contrast between tension and relaxation. If you are worried about other things, please put those aside for a while. Today, we are going to practice paying attention to how we feel. Sometimes our bodies let us know how we feel before our minds do. Please do not talk. I will be asking you questions, but think about the answers and keep your answers to yourself.

   We are now ready to begin. Please follow my directions exactly and concentrate on what you are feeling. First, close your eyes. Keeping your eyes closed, sit in your chair so that you feel comfortable. Think to yourself, how am I sitting? Are my legs stretched out or are they crossed? Are my arms at my side or folded? Am I sitting up straight or slouching? Think about how you are sitting and how you feel right now. (PAUSE FOR A FEW SECONDS.) Keeping your eyes closed, next make a frown with your face. Frown as much as you can. Frown harder . . . harder. Keep frowning and as you frown, think about how your face feels. Does it hurt? How do your eyebrows feel? How do your cheeks feel? How does your mouth feel? Okay, stop frowning. Keeping your eyes closed, think about how your face feels now. Does it feel different from when you were frowning? How do your eyebrows feel? Keeping your eyes closed, think about how your face feels now. Does it feel different from when you were frowning? How do your eyebrows feel? How do your cheeks feel? How does your mouth feel?

   Now, keeping your eyes closed, ball both hands into a fist. Ball the fists as tightly as you can and place your arms down at your sides, keeping your fists balled tightly. Think about how you feel right now. How do your fingers feel? How do your arms feel? How do your shoulders feel? (PAUSE FOR A FEW SECONDS.) Now unball your fists and relax. Keeping your eyes closed, think about how you feel right now. How do your fingers feel? How do your arms feel? How do your shoulders feel? Do you feel different now from how you did when you had your fists balled tightly? Think about how you felt with your fists balled and how you feel now. (PAUSE FOR A FEW SECONDS.)

Now, keeping your eyes closed, inhale and, as you inhale, try to hold in your stomach until it touches your back. Think about how you feel right now. How does your chest feel? How does your stomach feel? Exhale and relax. Think about how you feel right now. How does your chest feel? How does your stomach feel? Do you feel different now from how you did when you were holding your breath? (PAUSE FOR A FEW SECONDS.)

Now, keeping your eyes closed, stretch your legs out in front of you. Curl your toes under as tightly as you can. Think about how you feel right now. How do your toes feel? How do your legs feel? Do they hurt? Now uncurl your toes, unstretch your legs, and relax. Keeping your eyes closed, think about how you feel right now. How do your toes feel? How do your legs feel? Do they hurt? Think about how you felt with your toes curled under and your legs stretched and how you feel now. (PAUSE FOR A FEW SECONDS.)

Now, keeping your eyes closed, make a frown with your face. Ball your fists as tightly as you can, and place your arms down at your sides; hold in your breath and hold in your stomach until it touches your back. Stretch your legs out in front of you and curl your toes. Keeping eyes closed, think about how you feel right now. Okay, exhale, but keep the frown on your face, your fists balled, your legs stretched, and your toes curled. Think about how you feel right now. Okay, stop frowning, but keep your fists balled, your legs stretched, and your toes curled. Think about how you feel right now. Okay, unball your fists, but keep your legs stretched and your toes curled. Think about how you feel right now. Okay, now relax your legs and toes. Think about how you feel right now. Keep your eyes closed. Think about how your face feels. Think about how your shoulders feel. Think about how your arms feel. Think about how your shoulders feel. Think about how your fingers feel. Think about how your chest feels. Think about how your stomach feels. Think about how your legs feel. Think about how your toes feel. Keep your eyes closed and relax. Now open your eyes.

2. Have the trainees draw a picture of both relaxation and tension. You may even want them to color the pictures.
3. Ask the trainees to answer questions about the images.

4. Lead a discussion with questions from the trainees' worksheets.

5. Have pictures shared by those who are willing.

6. Try to communicate the idea of using images to feel relaxed.

7. Lead a discussion on how both relaxation and tension relieve stress.

Application for Trainees After the Group Meeting

1. Ask the trainees to think about their image of relaxation and imagine this at least twice a day.

2. Have them read and prepare for Exercise 15.6.

EXERCISE 15.6
DEEP BREATHING

Goal

To provide an opportunity for trainees to experience deep breathing

Introduction to the Exercise

Ask the trainees to get comfortable. Put on relaxing music and explain how deep breathing can actually change brain chemistry and reduce stress.

Training Procedures

1. Get very quiet.

2. Take them through counting by breathing in through the nose at the count of 3 and out at the count of 10. Repeat 10 times.

3. At the end say, "I feel calm and relaxed."

Application for Trainees After the Group Meeting

1. Ask trainees to practice deep breathing at least once a day.
2. Ask trainees to write about the impact of deep breathing.
3. Ask trainees to teach deep breathing to at least one other person.

EXERCISE 15.7
STRATEGIES FOR COPING WITH STRESS

Goal

To provide the trainees with tools for the management of stress

Introduction to the Exercise

Ask the trainees to get comfortable. Put on relaxing music and explain how deep breathing can actually change brain chemistry and reduce stress.

Training Procedures

1. Review the tools listed and take one to put into practice.
2. Ask them to discuss each of these and what might work for them.

Application for Trainees After the Group Meeting

Ask trainees to put one tool into practice.

EXERCISE 15.8
BALANCED, HEALTHY LIFE

Goal

To provide an opportunity for trainees to look at how balanced their lives are and to examine how they may want to change their lives

Introduction to the Exercise

Ask trainees to think about their life, and about a balance toward a healthier lifestyle. The trainer should describe several examples, so that trainees understand the concept of balance. Only when we manage stress at all levels of our lives are we able to move toward wellness.

Training Procedures

1. Review goals from Exercises 15.4, 15.5, and 15.6, and answer any questions.
2. Explain that today the training will involve looking at the "total you" to see if anything is out of balance.
3. Optional: Ask one trainee to stand in the middle of a circle. Have another representing "diet" move clockwise around the circle. Ask another trainee to move counterclockwise representing "emotional." Proceed until everyone is moving in either a clockwise or counterclockwise direction and then ask the "physical" to sit down. Ask the others to stop and discuss with them the interaction of all areas and what happens when one part stops.
4. Ask trainees to think about their own lives.
    - Are they eating balanced meals?
    - Are they feeling good most of the time?
    - Are they getting adequate exercise (vigorous exercise three times a week)?
    - Are they feeling okay psychologically?
    - Are they able to think and concentrate and problem solve?
    - Are they living in a healthy environment?
    - Do they have supportive friends and family?
    - Do they have a spiritual outlet?
    - Additional questions?
5. Ask trainees to set goals to deal with an area that is out of balance. They should not work on more than one area at a time.

Example: "I will exercise three times a week by running two miles each time."

Application for Trainees After the Group Meeting

1. Ask trainees to work on their goal.
2. Assign Exercise 15.9.

EXERCISE 15.9
HEALTH HABITS AS A MEANS OF REDUCING STRESS

Goal

To help the trainees get in touch with their lifestyles and examine ways to change their lifestyles

Introduction to the Exercise

The way we choose to live and how we handle stress and tension has a lot to do with how long we live. The trainee book includes a checklist to help trainees get in touch with some simple ways to change their lives.

Training Procedures

1. Review the homework from the previous exercise.
2. Show a DVD that looks at issues of wellness and healthy lifestyles.
3. Lead a discussion on health habits.
4. Lead a discussion on how to help the trainees change their lives.

Application for Trainees After the Group Meeting

1. Ask trainees to develop a plan of action for life change.
2. Assign Exercise 15.10.

EXERCISE 15.10
THOUGHTS, FEELINGS, BEHAVIOR

Goals

To assist the trainees in understanding the differences among thoughts, feelings, and behavior

To help the trainees understand how thoughts affect feelings and behavior

Introduction to the Exercise

When trainees and others are involved in a tense situation, trainees need to understand that they have a choice in terms of how they behave. Their behavior is influenced by thoughts and feelings. It is vital for them to understand that they can change their thoughts and, hence, their behavior.

Training Procedures

1. Review the homework from the last exercise.
2. Review the differences among thoughts, feelings, and behavior.

    A = Thoughts

    B = Feelings

    C = Behavior

    A + B = C

3. Demonstrate two alternative ways of thinking and feeling and behaving with practice rounds.
4. Divide the group into triads and continue the role-playing situations along with other situations that they may want to introduce themselves. Then ask them to write their thoughts, feelings, and behavior as well as alternative thoughts, feelings, and behavior.
5. While observing the role-playing activities, identify trainees who have particular strengths in making up dialogues that illustrate the situations accurately. Assist them, if needed.

Additional practice sessions could be established with the trainees' own examples.

6. Lead a discussion centered around:

   a. Do you see that the way we think about a situation often determines how we act?

   b. Do you understand that we all choose to behave in a certain way?

7. Have the trainees identify strong feelings in their personal life and come up with feelings and behavior.

Application for Trainees After the Group Meeting

1. Ask the trainees to identify strong feelings and thoughts by writing them down. Have them consider alternative thoughts and feelings.

2. Assign Exercise 15.11.

EXERCISE 15.11
EXAMINING YOUR SUPPORT SYSTEM

Goal

To enable the trainees to understand the need for a good support system

Introduction to the Exercise

This exercise is designed to help trainees learn about support systems and the help they can give, how to expand their own support system, how to make opportunities to give their support system a chance, and how they can support others.

Training Procedures

1. Review the homework from the previous exercise.

2. Discuss the fact that we all have "people needs," and that no one is self-sufficient, although some need people more than others do.

3. Ask the trainees to make lists of individuals with whom they have contact, and what need(s) they meet.
4. Ask the trainees to call out the needs that they have listed from their right-hand column on the chart "Your Needs and Your Support System" as you put them on the board.
5. Review the lists and show that they generally fall into the following categories:
   a. Physical Needs: sex, food, shelter
   b. Psychological Needs: caring, understanding, listening, intimacy
   c. Social Needs: belonging status, group identity, helping others
6. Lead the trainees through a discussion concerning how often they see those individuals whom they feel they need, who makes contact, and is there a pattern?
7. Explore the next section in terms of improving the effectiveness of individual support systems by planning a support system so that one's needs do not go unmet.
8. Discuss the three columns described in the chart in their workbooks. The first column of the chart is the type of support that individuals need, the second column is one for work and school, and the third column relates to personal life. Each of the three columns is divided into "Present" and "Possible."
9. Ask the trainees to brainstorm possible individuals who might provide support.
10. Focus on others we try to support and what function we play in terms of meeting others' needs.

Application for Trainees After the Group Meeting

1. Ask the trainees to write a paragraph concerning how to expand their own support system, as well as how they can be supportive of others.
2. Ask trainees to read Exercise 15.12.

EXERCISE 15.12
HOW TO BEAT STRESS

Goal

To provide a long-range plan to handle stress in a healthy manner

Introduction to the Exercise

How we choose to handle stress is an important factor of our well-being. Work with trainees to help them handle stress more effectively. It may be desirable to take them through a relaxation exercise.

Training Procedures

1. Review goals from Exercise 15.11 and previous exercises.
2. Ask trainees to review the list of how to beat stress.
3. Ask trainees to go through a relaxation activity. Have them sit comfortably with their eyes closed as the trainer slowly reads the following exercise. Ask them to quietly repeat each statement when finished.

Relaxation phrases:

a. I feel quiet.

b. I am beginning to feel relaxed.

c. The muscles in my toes and feet feel heavy and relaxed.

d. The muscles in my calves, knees, thighs, and hips feel heavy and relaxed.

e. My abdomen, solar plexus, and the whole central portion of my body feel heavy, relaxed, and comfortable.

f. My fingers, hands, arms, and shoulders feel heavy, relaxed, and comfortable.

g. My neck, jaws, eyes, and forehead feel relaxed. They feel comfortable and smooth.

h. The muscles in my whole body feel heavy, comfortable, relaxed, and quiet.

i. Continue silently on your own, feeling this heaviness throughout the body and continuing the relaxation (take 1 to 2 minutes).

j. I am quiet and relaxed.

k. My arms (legs) and hands (feet) feel heavy and warm.

l. I feel quiet.

m. My whole body is relaxed and my hands (feet) feel warm—relaxed and warm.

n. I can feel the warmth flowing down my arms (legs) into my hands (feet).

o. My hands are warm—toasty warm.

p. Warmth is flowing into my hands (feet); they are warm—very warm.

q. My hands (feet) are warm—relaxed and warm.

r. Continue silently on your own, feeling this warmth in the hands (feet) and fingers (toes) (take 1 to 2 minutes).

s. My whole body feels relaxed and my mind is quiet.

t. I have withdrawn my attention from the outside world, and I feel serene and still.

u. My attention is turned inward, and I feel at ease.

v. Within my mind I can visualize, imagine, and experience myself as relaxed, comfortable, and still.

w. I am aware in an easy, quiet, inward-turned way.

x. My mind is calm and quiet.

y. I feel an inward quietness.

z. I am at peace; I am at peace.

Continue silently on your own, feeling your body as relaxed and feeling your mind as calm, quiet, and peaceful (take 1 to 2 minutes).

The relaxation is now concluded, and the whole body is reactivated with a deep breath and the following phrases: (a) I feel life and energy flowing through my toes, feet, calves, knees, thighs, hips, solar plexus, chest, shoulders, arms, hands, fingers, neck, jaws, eyes, and head; (b) this energy makes me feel light and alive; (c) I open my eyes and make contact with the outside world; (d) I feel refreshed and good. (Stretch if desired.)

4. Ask the trainees how they felt.
5. Ask them to identify a long-range goal. Have them fill out the long-range goal forms. Have the whole group listen to the goals and as trainer makes comments.

Application for Trainees After the Group Meeting

1. Ask trainees to begin to implement a long-range goal.
2. Assign Exercise 15.13.

EXERCISE 15.13
LONG-RANGE GOALS

Goal

To help the trainees set up long-range goals in terms of changing their lifestyle

Introduction to the Exercise

Help trainees know the importance of developing their goals. Provide trainees with group assistance to set up specific activities to accomplish long-range goals.

Training Procedures

1. Review the homework from the previous exercise.
2. Ask the trainees to address long-range goals for themselves in terms of mental, physical, and emotional aspects.

3. Use the last sheet in their workbooks for this module to expand on their goal(s).

4. Divide the group into twos and review their long-range goal(s).

5. Ask the trainees to have you review those goals.

6. Discuss how a support system could assist them in reaching these goals.

Application for Trainees After the Group Meeting

1. Ask trainees to read the introduction to Module XVI.
2. Assign Exercise 16.1.

MODULE

MENTAL HEALTH AWARENESS AND REFERRAL

Goal

To help trainees understand the importance of good mental health

Approximate Time

Module Introduction

Application—10 to 15 minutes

Exercise 16.1—60 to 90 minutes in training session

Application—15 minutes

Exercise 16.2—60 minutes in training session

Application—15 minutes

Exercise 16.3—30 to 60 minutes in training session

Application—15 minutes

Exercise 16.4—30 to 60 minutes in training session

Application—15 minutes

Exercise 16.5—30 to 60 minutes in training session

Application—30 minutes

Materials

- *Peer Power, Book Two, Workbook* (one copy for each trainee)

Introduction to the Module

Mental health is vital. For example, according to the World Health Organization, mental health is the number one reason for workplace disability. Learning how to recognize mental health issues and seek help for the issues is essential to ensure healthy employable people. Over the years, mental health issues have been difficult for people to recognize and admit to. Part of the purpose of this module is to get rid of the stigma in seeking professional help for mental health issues.

Training Procedures

1. Determine the number of training sessions needed, and the exercises to be included in each session.
2. Review the content to be covered and the suggested activities as listed in *Peer Power, Book Two, Workbook*.
3. Be open and positive.
4. Seek out a local psychologist or counselor to assist you in Exercise 16.1.
5. You may want to use J.10 from the CD in *Peer Programs* for a reflection evaluation.
6. You may want to use J.11 to plan activities to inform others concerning good mental health.

Evaluation Process

Evaluate the process used in teaching this skill by the feedback you obtain from the trainees and by observing them interacting in the group.

Measuring Outcomes

1. Use Exercise 16.1 to determine whether or not trainees can relate personally to any of the mental health issues.

2. Use Exercise 16.2 to determine whether or not trainees can use the examples and make appropriate professional referrals.

3. Use Exercise 16.3 to help trainees determine how to inform others of the importance of maintaining good mental health.

EXERCISE 16.1
RECOGNIZING COMMON MENTAL HEALTH ISSUES

Goals

To assist trainees in understanding common mental health issues

To identify mental health issues in the peer helpers group and in others

Introduction to the Exercise

The purpose of this exercise is to review common mental health issues. Your focus is not to diagnose the peer helpers or others they know, but to share information about mental health issues. This exercise would be enhanced by asking a local psychologist or school counselor to facilitate the exercise. With the learning disability section, you may want to ask a special education instructor to help.

Training Procedures

1. Review the introduction and the section on a variety of common mental health issues.

2. Ask the trainees to share where they have observed these mental health issues.

3. Ask them to think about how they can help others with these issues.

4. Ask trainees to research local resources that provide mental health help, either through insurance or reduced fees. Have the provider's names available as resources to the participants.

Application for Trainees After the Group Meeting

1. Ask trainees to become aware of mental health issues, either through reading articles or reviewing the Internet.
2. Ask trainees to read and review Exercise 16.2.

EXERCISE 16.2
HOW TO RECOGNIZE OTHERS WITH MENTAL HEALTH ISSUES

Goals

To help identify those with mental health issues

To raise awareness of mental health issues

Introduction to the Exercise

It is important that the trainees apply what they have learned in Exercise 16.1 and share the issues in each of the situations with others in the group. It is important to apply what they have learned earlier and to begin having the trainees discuss how to get rid of the stigma of seeking professional help for mental health issues.

Training Procedures

1. Review the application activity from the last exercise.
2. Discuss how to raise awareness of mental health issues.
3. Ask the trainees to get into small groups to discuss different mental health issues. Ask them to discuss what action they could take for each issue.
4. Ask each group to summarize their discussions for the total group. If time is an issue, assign one example to each group.

Application for Trainees After the Group Meeting

1. Ask trainees to describe each issue in writing, and how the issue may apply to their own experiences.
2. Ask trainees to read and review Exercise 16.3.

EXERCISE 16.3
HOW TO REFER OTHERS WITH MENTAL HEALTH ISSUES

Goals

To assist trainees in learning how to refer others for mental health help

To practice making mental health referrals

Introduction to the Exercise

Review the steps in making a referral. It is important to demonstrate the referral steps first before asking the peer helpers to practice the steps. Review skills from *Peer Power, Book One*, such as empathy, attending, and problem solving, and demonstrate how to use these skills in the practice section.

Training Procedures

1. Review the steps required for peer helping.
2. Place the trainees into small groups of three to practice utilizing the examples from Exercise 16.2. Continue practicing until all members have been a helper, helpee, and observer.
3. Discuss the observer's feedback that describes what went well and what could have gone better.

Application for Trainees After the Group Meeting

1. Ask the trainees to write about their experience and reflect upon Exercise 16.3.
2. Ask the trainees to be prepared to talk about how to raise others' awareness concerning mental health.

EXERCISE 16.4
HOW TO RAISE AWARENESS
CONCERNING MENTAL HEALTH

Goal

To help trainees develop ideas of how to raise others' awareness on the topic of mental health

Introduction to the Exercise

This exercise is an important tool to put ideas of how to raise awareness of mental health in others into action. You may want to have the trainees brainstorm and deliver the information regarding mental health mental issues to others.

Training Procedures

1. Review the writing and reflections about the trainees' reaction to Exercise 16.3.
2. Assign the trainees to small groups to brainstorm mental health activities that can be shared with others.
3. Follow the plan of action.
4. Ask trainees (as a total group) to have a project to deliver regarding mental health.
5. Directions 4 and 5 in the student workbook are about evaluation of the activity.

Application for Trainees After the Group Meeting

Ask trainees to deliver an awareness activity to others.

MODULE

LEADERSHIP TRAINING

Goals

To enable trainees to examine their leadership style

To assist trainees in developing techniques for leading a group, including development of action plans and planning a meeting

Approximate Time

Module Introduction

Application—10 to 15 minutes of homework

Exercise 17.1—60 minutes in training session

Exercise 17.2—60 to 90 minutes in training session

Application—30 minutes

Exercise 17.3—60 to 90 minutes in training session

Application—30 minutes

Exercise 17.4—60 minutes in training session

Application—60 minutes

Exercise 17.5—30 minutes in training session

Exercise 17.6—60 minutes in training session

Application—30 minutes

Exercise 17.7—60 to 90 minutes in training session

Exercise 17.8—60 to 90 minutes in training session

Application—30 minutes

Materials

- *Peer Power, Book Two, Workbook* (one copy for each trainee)
- Optional: If this module is used with an existing organization, the trainer may want to use the organization's own activities for work in Exercises 17.5, 17.6, and 17.7.

Introduction to the Module

Many individuals who lack the necessary skills to do a good job are often called upon to serve in leadership roles. This is frustrating for the group and for the leader. This module will assist in helping trainees identify their own leadership styles and learn some practical ideas that will help them be effective leaders.

Training Procedures

1. Decide on how to group the activities.
2. Decide if it is desired to use the organization's issues.
3. Move from group to group to give feedback.

Evaluation Process

Evaluate the process through feedback from participants and from written work.

Measuring Outcomes

1. Use Exercise 17.1 to measure leadership style.
2. Use Exercises 17.2 and 17.3 to assess discussion group skills.

3. Use Exercise 17.4 to assess time management skills.
4. Use Exercises 17.5, 17.6, and 17.7 to actually set up a plan of action.
5. Use Exercise 17.8 to help the trainees identify their leadership purpose.

EXERCISE 17.1
LEADERSHIP STYLE PROFILE

Goal

To help trainees assess their own leadership styles

Introduction to the Exercise

The leadership style exercise helps individuals discover the kind of leaders they are, either task-oriented or people-oriented. The following activities will assist reviewing the differences between the two.

Training Procedures

1. Discuss the different types of leaders—those who are democratic, *laissez-faire*, or autocratic.
2. You may want trainees to practice the different types.
3. Have trainees fill out the "T-P Leadership Questionnaire."
4. Discuss the importance of combined concern for task and person.
5. Participants will score their own questionnaires on the dimensions of task orientation (T) and people orientation (P) in order to locate themselves on the "Leadership Style Profile" sheet.
6. Explain the following scoring guide:
    a. Circle the number for items 8, 12, 17, 18, 19, 30, 34, and 35.
    b. Write a 1 in front of the circled items to which you responded S (seldom) or N (never).

c. Write a 1 in front of items not circled to which you responded A (always) or F (frequently).

d. Count the circled 1s. This is your score for concern for people. Record this number in the blank following the letter P.

e. Count the uncircled 1s. This is your score for concern for task. Record this number in the blank following the letter T.

7. Ask the trainees to follow directions on the profile sheet. Lead a discussion of the implications that members attach to their location on the profile.

Application for Trainees After the Group Meeting

1. Ask trainees to think about the types of leadership observed and decide if they are task-oriented or people-oriented leaders.

2. Ask trainees to read the information in Exercise 17.2.

EXERCISE 17.2
LEADING A DISCUSSION GROUP

Goal

To experience leading a small discussion group and receiving feedback

Introduction to the Exercise

Leaders are often asked to lead discussion groups. This exercise will assist the trainee in leading a discussion group.

Training Procedures

1. Ask for feedback from Exercise 17.1.

2. Have trainees divide into small discussion groups.

3. Ask one person to be an observer and use the observation form.
4. Move among discussion groups and give leaders feedback.
5. Continue until everyone has been both a discussion leader and an observer.

Application for Trainees After the Group Meeting

Look over Exercise 17.3.

EXERCISE 17.3
WORKING WITH OTHERS

Goal

To assist the trainees in understanding how they relate to others who are different from themselves and to develop the ability to work with others who have different strengths. They also experience practice in motivating others in a group meeting.

Introduction to the Exercise

The ability to understand and work with others different from ourselves is an important skill. Individuals often withdraw from and are afraid of those who are different. This exercise will take trainees through a role-play situation.

Training Procedures

1. Review previous homework.
2. Ask the trainees to identify and think about some people they know who are different from them.
   a. Do they get along with them?
   b. Are they threatened?
3. Take the trainees through an example of different types of individuals.
4. Lead a practice group with different types of individuals portrayed.

5. Use the practice example in *Peer Power, Book Two, Workbook* to help them think of team members.

    Example: Outgoing individuals of different cultures—someone good with accounting and money—someone good at setting up an exact plan.

6. Have a group practice the example. This will necessitate roles for each, including identifying the leader.
7. Following the practice round, discuss the actions of the leader, help the group understand positive aspects, and identify other things that might have been done, if any.
8. Change roles so that all of the members have a chance to lead.

Application for Trainees After the Group Meeting

1. Have the trainees think of a group that they presently lead and decide how to work with those individuals who are different from themselves.
2. Have them prepare for the next exercise.

EXERCISE 17.4
TIME MANAGEMENT

Goal

To help the trainees look at time wasters and how they spend their present time

Introduction to the Exercise

Often leaders are ineffective because they cannot get things done. This exercise will help you look at the time management skills of the trainees and suggest ways to change them. Focus on time wasted on the Internet and on video games.

Training Procedures

1. Discuss different time wasters.
2. Discuss ways that they can change some of their time wasters.

3. Help the trainees look at the long-term and short-term goals that they have set for themselves. Goals might include the following:

   Long-term goals:
   a. Going to college
   b. Being a good parent
   c. Becoming a pilot

   Short-term goals:
   d. Losing weight
   e. Quitting smoking

3. Ask the trainees to make a list of activities for yesterday.
4. Ask them to account for the approximate time that it took.
5. Ask the trainees to indicate whether the activities were "have to" or "want to." Ask them to notice the balance.
6. Ask whether the activities fit into short-term or long-term goals.
7. Ask the trainees to develop a plan to manage their time differently.

Application for Trainees After the Group Meeting

1. Ask trainees to keep a chart of how they spend your time.
2. Ask trainees to keep a journal of how to address time utilization problems.
3. Ask trainees to learn to prioritize activities.
4. Ask trainees to look for a balance of "have to" and "want to."

EXERCISE 17.5
DEVELOPING AN ACTION PLAN

Goal

To assist trainees in developing their own action plan for a leadership position

Introduction to the Exercise

This activity will help trainees focus on how to establish what needs to be done in certain leadership positions.

Training Procedures

1. Ask for feedback from Exercise 17.4.
2. Have the trainees work in groups of two to develop their own action plan.
3. If they do not have assigned leadership positions or cannot think of one, assign one.
4. Work with the groups in developing the plan.
5. Collect the action plans for written feedback.

Application for Trainees After the Group Meeting

1. Ask trainees to complete the action plan at home, if not done during the session.
2. Ask trainees to complete Exercise 17.6 for homework.

EXERCISE 17.6
PLANNING PUBLIC RELATIONS

Goals

To assist trainees in following through with their plans for Exercise 17.5

To plan for public relations

Introduction to the Exercise

Leaders must keep their publics—membership, coworkers, community, organization officials—informed of plans, needs, and activities. To do so requires careful planning well in advance, with responsibilities clearly delineated. Approval must be obtained before implementation of the plan, as well as assurance of financial and other necessary resources. The leader is responsible for making sure that the public relations aspect is integrated early and throughout the action.

Training Procedures

1. Return material from Exercise 17.5 with comments. These sheets are to be used in Exercise 17.6.
2. Ask trainees to share homework from Exercise 17.6 and share comments that might help each other.
3. Divide the group to work in pairs and ask them to assist each other in improving their public relations plans.
4. Using a local and specific example, identify the different publics and their needs for different kinds of information about an organization or a business.
5. Collect the written plans.
6. Have trainees share experiences from working on their plans as partners and answer questions.

Application for Trainees After the Group Meeting

Ask trainees to complete Exercise 17.7 for the next meeting.

EXERCISE 17.7
PLANNING A CONFERENCE OR OTHER MEETINGS

Goal

To teach trainees how to plan a conference or other meetings

Introduction to the Exercise

Planning a conference or other meetings is a big part of leadership. The following exercise will take the trainees through the process.

Training Procedures

1. Write down the people and task issues in a conference.
2. Establish conference or meeting particulars such as title, format, place and time, speakers or presenters.
3. Coordinate your organizational and operational assistance—list those individuals who will help, the external and internal contacts, and sources of materials.
4. Ask trainees to work in clusters of three to plan a conference.
5. Return material from Exercise 17.6 and make comments.
6. Ask if there are any problems with application from Exercise 17.7.
7. Ask trainees to share homework for Exercise 17.7 and make suggestions.

Application for Trainees After the Exercise

1. Ask the trainees to finalize a plan for a conference.
2. Ask the trainees to reflect on this exercise through writing in a journal.

EXERCISE 17.8
BE A PURPOSE-DRIVEN LEADER

Goal

To help the trainees articulate their purpose as a leader

Introduction to the Exercise

It is important that leaders can articulate their purpose for the activity they are leading. Those leaders who demonstrate purpose are more effective in accomplishing their vision and mission.

Training Procedures

1. Assist the trainees in identifying their personal purpose for taking on this project/activity/issue.
2. Help trainees identify whether the event/thought/behavior experienced has led them to the intended purpose.
3. Ask trainees to state how they will know if the purpose has been accomplished.
4. Discuss issues from previous exercise.
5. Collect the written plans.
6. Ask teams to share their plan with the entire training group. Offer suggestions.

Application for the Trainee After the Group Meeting

Ask trainees to review the introduction to Module XVIII: Peer Helping Through Tutoring.

MODULE

PEER HELPING THROUGH TUTORING

Goals

To help trainees master material related to motivation

To help trainees recognize their own ability to tutor others

To help trainees understand their own study habits

To help trainees develop their own way of learning

To help trainees learn specific skills to tutor individuals in problem areas

To help trainees learn how to deal with problem areas

To help trainees develop techniques to be a successful tutor

Approximate Time

Module Introduction—10 to 15 minutes for homework

Exercise 18.1—60 to 120 minutes in training session
Application—30 minutes

Exercise 18.2—30 to 60 minutes in training session
Application—30 minutes

Exercise 18.3—30 to 60 minutes in training session
Application—120 minutes

Exercise 18.4—120 to 160 minutes in training session
Application—120 minutes

Exercise 18.5—30 to 60 minutes in training session
Application—30 minutes

Exercise 18.6—30 to 60 minutes in training session
Application—20 minutes

Exercise 18.7—30 to 60 minutes in training session
Application—20 minutes

Exercise 18.8—30 to 60 minutes in training session
Application—20 minutes

Exercise 18.9—60 to 120 minutes in training session
Application—30 minutes

Materials

- *Peer Power, Book Two, Workbook* (one copy for each trainee)
- Optional: DVD or CD on study skills
- Speaker: Ask someone from special education (an L.D. or B.D. teacher) to talk to the trainees about how to manage tutees with special needs.

Introduction to the Module

Tutoring can be one of the most rewarding roles a peer helper can perform. It is very important that the peer tutor has completed *Peer Power, Book One* before starting on this module. Most schools have a service learning program, which often involves older peers tutoring younger peers. Many high schools provide tutor/mentoring to ninth graders. Before peer tutors/mentors are able to help tutees, training is critical as well as supervision. Planning for reflection time can help to integrate the skill.

You may want to expand on this module if this is the only role that your trainees will perform. You may want to include different material if they will be working with very young children or adults. The exercises and information from this unit also can be used with the tutee. The material is not designed to help tutors who are working with students with severe learning problems. These students may require professional tutors.

Training Procedures

1. Select the number of training sessions and exercises to be included in this module.

2. Be prepared to demonstrate all of the practice situations. If you don't feel comfortable, ask a professional teacher to demonstrate some of these situations.

3. If a speaker is used, arrange for it to be with the appropriate exercise.

4. The homework portion of this module is important and should be reviewed carefully.

5. When actually practicing tutoring, the management of the sessions becomes very important. Gaining support of the cooperating teacher regarding issues such as where to conduct the tutoring, support for the tutor, and materials is critical.

Evaluation Process

You can evaluate the process used in teaching a skill by the practice used by the trainees and the written homework.

Use J.10 on reflection from the CD of *Peer Programs*.

Measuring Outcomes

1. Use Exercise 18.5 in terms of integration of skills.

2. Use Exercise 18.6 in terms of tutoring operation.

EXERCISE 18.1
SELF-ASSESSMENT

Goals

To provide the trainees an opportunity to assess their own ability to tutor

To review the introductory material

Introduction to the Exercise

The following assessment can be used before starting the module, and at the conclusion. You may want to supplement the introduction section with a DVD or CD to provide activities on motivation or learning.

Training Procedures

1. Review the material from the introduction as well as the reaction of the trainees to the DVD or CD.
2. Discuss motivation and Maslow's needs in relationship to the trainee's level of need (e.g., level of love needs). Use the introduction material to Module XVIII, *Peer Power, Book Two, Workbook*.
3. Discuss the difference between encouraging and discouraging statements.
4. Help the trainees complete the "Self-Assessment Questionnaire" and recognize the strengths that they have now as tutors.
5. Help the trainees set goals for improving weaknesses; use the entire group to brainstorm goals.
6. Have each trainee complete the goal sheet (last page of Exercise 18.1). Talk with them individually, and when the plan is appropriate, sign the goal sheet to show your approval. (This may need to be completed at the next meeting with the group.)

Application for Trainees After the Group Meeting

1. Ask the trainees to fill out the goal sheet, if not completed, and review with them any additional ideas that you may have.
2. Have the trainees prepare for Exercise 18.2.

EXERCISE 18.2
HOW I STUDY

Goals

To help the trainees understand their own study habits

To help the trainees develop a plan to improve their own study habits

Introduction to the Exercise

Discuss with trainees the need to understand their own values and their own ways of studying. Then, discuss how they can use their strengths to help others, and how they can learn new ways to study.

Trainees also may want to use this with their own tutee once a relationship has been established.

Training Procedures

1. Discuss the trainees' homework assignment.
2. Review the total scores on the "Personal Study Habits Survey."
3. Assist the trainees in recognizing their strengths and weaknesses.
4. Assign homework to develop a plan. You may want to spend class time to get them started.

Application for Trainees After the Group Meeting

1. Develop a plan for change.
2. Bring back for review.
3. Prepare for Exercise 18.3.

EXERCISE 18.3
HOW I LEARN BEST

Goals

To help trainees understand their preferred way of learning

To help the trainees apply this information to how they study

To help the trainees apply this information to tutoring

Introduction to the Exercise

We all have a way of learning that we prefer. However, we need to develop additional learning styles. Be sure to be clear about these different learning styles and also about developing additional ways of learning. Use a lecturer and/or audiovisual materials.

Training Procedures

1. Include "Styles of Learning" in your lecture.
2. Provide examples and have the trainees brainstorm examples. Have them share how they learn.

    Examples:
    - Big picture making
    - Making a connection to something else

3. Have the trainees take and score the "Learning Style Survey."
4. Discuss the results of the survey.
5. Lead the group to cover "Discussion Questions."

6. Make the point that there is no right way to learn.

7. Work with the trainees to show them ways to do their homework.

Application for Trainees After the Group Meeting

1. Ask the trainees to design and plan tutoring someone using each style.

2. Ask the trainees to use this skill in teaching various content areas.

3. Ask the trainees to prepare for Exercise 18.4.

Styles of Learning

Visual learning: Student learns by watching, likes to read, has good imagination, shows emotions facially, usually legible penmanship, dresses neatly, plans and outlines, takes good notes, and likes order and tidiness.

Auditory learning: Student learns by listening, likes to discuss, remembers by reciting, will move lips while reading silently, likes quiet, is distracted by outside noise, and displays emotion through intonation.

Kinesthetic learning: Student learns by doing, needs to be directly involved, likes to move around during study, appears impulsive, shows emotion, uses hands when talking, and does not tend toward order and neatness.

Examples of visual tutoring:

- Write an outline
- Have tutee take notes

Examples of auditory tutoring:

- Read directions out loud
- Talk to tutee about work
- Tape-record important things

Examples of kinesthetic tutoring:

- Hands-on activity
- Encourage writing
- Trace new words

EXERCISE 18.4
MAJOR STUDY SKILLS

Goals

To teach the SQ3R method, test-taking, note-taking, writing skills, and time management

To have trainees practice these skills

Introduction to the Exercise

This exercise may take three to four class periods to learn and practice. You may also want to invite a special education teacher to demonstrate some of these skills.

Training Procedures

1. Review the homework from the previous exercise.
2. Review the written material in this exercise.
3. Demonstrate each activity.
4. Have the trainees work in groups of three: One person is the tutor, one is the tutee, and one is the observer. The observer is to give feedback as to whether or not the tutor used the information in this exercise.
5. Have the trainees do the other activities identified in Directions 4 through 9 in the student workbook.

Application for Trainees After the Group Meeting

1. Ask the trainees to write the activities that they were not able to complete in the group work.
2. Ask the trainees to prepare for Exercise 18.5.

EXERCISE 18.5
UNDERSTANDING MISBEHAVIOR OF OTHERS

Goals

To review the four goals of misbehavior

To teach trainees strategies of coping with misbehavior

Introduction to the Exercise

Adlerian psychology has helped educators and parents to be more effective in working with youth who misbehave. You may want to invite a local psychologist or the school counselor to present this lesson.

Training Procedures

1. Review the information on the four goals of misbehavior.
2. Help the trainees identify examples of misbehavior.
3. Review strategies of how to manage the four goals of misbehavior.
4. Set up homework activities that allow trainees to observe and practice working with the behavior.

Application for Trainees After the Group Meeting

1. Ask the trainees to practice working with youth, and utilize some of the strategies.
2. Ask the trainees to practice with their friends or siblings to recognize the four goals and try some of the strategies.

EXERCISE 18.6
USING POSITIVE REINFORCERS FOR BEHAVIOR MANAGEMENT OF STUDENTS

Goals

To teach trainees how to reinforce behavior that is positive in tutoring

To help trainees develop their own reinforcers

Introduction to the Exercise

Using reinforcers to tutor others is a good tool for behavior management of tutees. The value is to discover the specific reinforcer that will motivate the tutee.

Training Procedures

1. Ask your trainees to think about someone they have tutored in the past or are currently tutoring. Have trainees describe the tutee and what kind of behavior the tutee exhibited during tutoring.
2. Help trainees identify one positive behavior that the tutee exhibited during the tutoring time.
3. Help trainees think of an example of a positive reinforcer the tutor might use.

Application for Trainees After the Group Meeting

1. Ask trainees to think about and develop one positive reinforcer for appropriate tutee behavior.
2. Have trainees design reinforcers to suit the individual tutee's needs.

EXERCISE 18.7
WILLIAM GLASSER: HOW TO DISCIPLINE

Goal

To review Glasser's approach to discipline and how this applies to the tutee

Introduction to the Exercise

Glasser has some excellent guidelines for disciplining students that can be applied to tutees. You may want to ask the trainees to present a report on Glasser's theories of discipline.

Training Procedures

1. Help the trainees review the seven steps for discipline that will apply to a tutee.
2. Help the trainee write a discipline plan for their tutee.

Application for Trainees After the Group Meeting

1. Ask trainees to think about issues in peer tutoring.
2. Have trainees describe in writing how to deal with these issues.

EXERCISE 18.8
PROBLEMS IN TUTORING

Goals

To help the trainees learn how to deal with special problems in tutoring

To help the trainees practice using skills in tutoring

Introduction to the Exercise

This exercise is used to integrate the skills used in *Peer Power, Book One* and in the earlier lessons of this module.

Training Procedures

1. Review the homework.
2. Demonstrate the following:
   - Attending
   - Empathy
   - Encouraging word
   - Contracting

3. Ask the tutors to work in groups of three. As you observe their role-playing, ask them to work on attending, empathy, responses, encouragement, and contracting.

4. Stop after completing each of the directions in the *Peer Power, Book Two, Workbook*, and discuss and give feedback.

5. Lead a final discussion.

Application for Trainees After the Group Meeting

1. Have the trainees complete (in writing) those items in the directions that were not completed in the group.

2. Ask the trainees to prepare for Exercise 18.9.

EXERCISE 18.9
PUTTING TUTORING SKILLS INTO ACTION

Goals

To review the steps involved in putting a tutoring program into action

To allow trainees to practice skills of tutoring

Introduction to the Exercise

You may want to emphasize each of the points listed on each step and apply these to your situation. Trainees may also want to take the self-assessment test again (Exercise 18.1).

Training Procedures

1. Review each of the steps.

2. Apply these to your local situation.

3. Demonstrate a tutoring experience.

4. Have the trainees divide into groups of three and practice tutoring. Have the observer fill out the observation sheet and share it with the trainee, who then gives it to you.

Application for Trainees After the Group Meeting

1. Ask trainees to set up a first meeting with cooperating teacher and tutee.
2. Ask trainees to react to the role-playing situation.
3. Assign reading of the introduction to Module XIX.

MODULE

PEER HELPING THROUGH GROUP WORK: PEER EDUCATION AND SUPPORT

Goal

To enable trainees to facilitate groups: small, classroom, or large groups

Approximate Time

Module Introduction

Application—10 to 15 minutes

Exercise 19.1—30 to 40 minutes in training session

Application—40 minutes

Exercise 19.2—60 to 120 minutes in training session

Application—20 minutes

Exercise 19.3—60 to 90 minutes in training session

Exercise 19.4—60 to 120 minutes in training session

Exercise 19.5—60 to 120 minutes in training session

Exercise 19.6—60 to 120 minutes in training session

Exercise 19.7—30 to 60 minutes in training session
Application—20 minutes for 1 week

Exercise 19.8—60 to 90 minutes in training session
Application—60 minutes

Exercise 19.9—30 to 60 minutes in training session
Application—30 minutes

Exercise 19.10—90 to 120 minutes in training session
Application—60 minutes

Exercise 19.11—60 minutes in training session
Application—30 minutes

Exercise 19.12—4 to 5 hours
Application—60 minutes

Materials

- *Peer Power, Book Two, Workbook* (one copy for each trainee)
- Optional: If this module is used with an existing organization, you may want to use your own activities in Exercises 19.4, 19.5, 19.6, and 19.12.

Introduction to the Module

Many organizations have now gone to participatory management; therefore, facilitating group skills is essential. Many companies are using quality circles. The education community utilizes small discussion groups to encourage prevention in specific areas of need and to help all participants in the group feel they belong. Churches are using the discussion format to assist their congregation to feel a part of the group and to have a voice in making relevant decisions. Peer helpers are called upon to lead large education groups on a variety of health and safety topics. This module will assist in training others in small and large group skills.

Training Procedures

1. Select the exercises to use for this module.
2. Determine if it is desirable to use your own organizational issues.
3. Move from group to group to give feedback.
4. Use this module along with Module XVII: Leadership Training.
5. Model each discussion before the trainees.
6. Once the peer helpers are trained in facilitating groups, design projects to use in either small or large group work (from elementary school age to adult to the elderly).

Evaluation Process

Evaluate the process used in teaching through the feedback from participants, as well as by their written work and evaluation materials.

Measuring Outcomes

1. Use Exercise 19.4 to measure skills in the life problems group (facilitating open-ended discussions).
2. Use Exercise 19.5 to measure skills in the subject matter group (facilitating discussions on specific topics).
3. Use Exercise 19.6 to measure skills in the decision-making (problem-solving) group (facilitating discussions related to tasks).
4. Use Exercise 19.7 both before and after the module to check for understanding.
5. Use the observation form from Exercise 19.12 to check on skill development.

6. Watch and listen closely during the practice sessions to determine the ease with which trainees are able to demonstrate this skill.

7. Use the reflection from J.10 of the CD in the *Peer Programs* book.

EXERCISE 19.1
SELF-ASSESSMENT OF GROUP FACILITATOR SKILLS

Goal

To help trainees assess their own group facilitator skills

Introduction to the Exercise

Group facilitation skills are difficult and involve skills in basic communication. The following exercise will assist trainees in reviewing their own perception of basic skills.

Training Procedures

1. Discuss each of the areas being assessed and give examples.
2. Discuss the following as basic conditions for a good small group discussion:
    a. Clear topic of interest to the group
    b. Group members differ in their opinions
    c. A climate of acceptance that promotes expression
    d. A facilitator who gets things going and then serves as a guide
3. Have the trainees take an assessment.
4. Discuss each area to gain additional ideas from the trainees.
5. Have the group members share their strengths and weaknesses.

Application for Trainees After the Group Meeting

1. Help the trainees find groups to participate in as an application assignment.
2. Ask trainees to prepare for Exercise 19.2.

EXERCISE 19.2
FUNCTIONS OF A DISCUSSION FACILITATOR

Goals

To help the trainees understand the different functions and activities involved in leading a group

To have trainees practice on small activities

Introduction to the Exercise

Peer helpers are often asked to facilitate small discussion groups. Before leading an entire group, it is helpful to first practice on small segments of group facilitation.

Training Procedures

1. Review all of the functions. Use the list provided in "Group Facilitator Functions" listed in *Peer Power, Book Two, Workbook*.
2. List the functions on chalkboard or flip chart.
3. Center a discussion around each area.
4. Demonstrate how to lead each section.

    Example: Dealing with problem participants (Number 5 in the "Group Facilitator Functions" list)

5. Have the trainees move into groups of four, with one observer. Have the facilitator of each group lead the discussion on just one issue (e.g., starting a group). Have the observer use the feedback form entitled "Discussion Skills

Observations." Then have the observer give feedback. Make sure that each group works on all of the issues. Rotate roles in the group.

Application for Trainees After the Group Meeting

1. Ask trainees to examine checklist from Exercise 19.1.
2. Ask trainees to prepare for Exercise 19.3.

EXERCISE 19.3
LEADING A DISCUSSION GROUP

Goal

To provide trainees the experience of leading a small discussion group and getting feedback in a small discussion group

Introduction to the Exercise

Leaders are often asked to facilitate a discussion group. This exercise will assist the trainee in facilitating a discussion group.

Training Procedures

1. Ask for feedback from Exercise 19.2.
2. Demonstrate what you are asking the trainees to do.
3. Have the trainees divide into small discussion groups.
4. Ask one person to be an observer and use the "Observer Evaluation Form."
5. Move among the different discussion groups, and give feedback to the facilitator.
6. Continue until everyone has been both a discussion leader and an observer.

Application for Trainees After the Group Meeting

1. Ask trainees to look over Exercise 19.1.
2. Ask trainees to prepare for Exercise 19.4.

EXERCISE 19.4
LIFE PROBLEMS GROUP

Goal

To have the trainees experience leading a rap group (life problems group)

Introduction to the Exercise

One of the most valuable benefits of participating in a peer counseling group is the sharing that takes place. This exercise will give participants an opportunity to share their own concerns or some from the stimulus questions entitled "Let's Discuss."

Training Procedures

1. Ask for feedback from the previous exercise.
2. Review the role of facilitator in this type of group.
3. Demonstrate how to lead a life problems group.
4. Divide into groups of five, with one facilitator, one observer, and three participants.
5. Have the observer focus on facilitator skills, using the "Group Feedback Form" provided. You may want to have the observer give the "Group Feedback Form" to the facilitator, who in turn will give it to you.

Application for Trainees After the Group Meeting

1. Have the trainees refer back to the skills listed in Exercise 19.1 and evaluate their own effectiveness.
2. Ask the trainees to prepare for Exercise 19.5.

EXERCISE 19.5
SUBJECT MATTER GROUP

Goal

To teach trainees to make presentations to topical groups

Introduction to the Exercise

Often, information that is presented by peers is far more accepted by the group members than those presented by the group leader; therefore, it would be helpful for your peer group facilitators to have various topics that they can discuss.

Training Procedures

1. Ask for feedback from Exercise 19.4.
2. Demonstrate leading a group before asking the trainees to lead a group.
3. Have the trainees divide into small discussion groups.
4. Ask one person to be a discussion facilitator and another person to be an observer and use an observation form.
5. Move among the discussion groups and give the facilitator feedback.
6. Continue until everyone has been both a discussion facilitator and an observer.
7. Focus on the group members.

Application for Trainees After the Group Meeting

1. Ask trainees to look over Exercise 19.1.
2. Ask trainees to prepare for Exercise 19.6.

EXERCISE 19.6
DECISION-MAKING GROUP

Goal

To help trainees experience leading a small group that needs to perform a task or arrive at a solution

Introduction to the Exercise

Facilitators are asked to help groups make decisions and solve problems. This exercise will assist the trainee with this type of group.

Training Procedures

1. Ask for feedback from Exercise 19.2.
2. Review the steps to problem solving (as outlined in Module XXII, *Peer Power, Book One*), and spend time having trainees discuss and understand brainstorming (see "Brainstorming" in *Peer Power, Book Two, Workbook,* Exercise 19.6).
3. Demonstrate how to lead a problem-solving group.
4. Have the trainees divide into small discussion groups and use one of the "Suggested Decisions To Be Made" or one that you give them.
5. Ask one person to be an observer and use the observation form and one person to be a facilitator.
6. Move among discussion groups and give the facilitator feedback.
7. Continue until everyone has been both a facilitator and an observer.

Application for Trainees After the Group Meeting

1. Ask trainees to look over Exercise 19.1.
2. Ask trainees to prepare for Exercise 19.7.

EXERCISE 19.7
CHECKLIST OF SKILLS FOR CLASSROOM GROUP

Goal

To teach trainees some of the skills needed for leading a classroom group, as compared to one-on-one helping and small group discussion

Introduction to the Exercise

In Exercise 19.7, the trainees will learn to differentiate among skills needed for a variety of helping roles. They also will become aware of the skills they need to improve on.

Training Procedures

1. Discuss the introductory material.
2. Have the trainees review together the "Skills of Helping" chart and discuss each point.
3. Be sure the trainees take note of those skills unique to a large classroom.
4. Have the trainees indicate whether each skill is a strength, if they possess the skill and feel comfortable in using it, or if they need help to develop it.
5. Have each trainee identify possible ways other members of the group might assist him/her in developing better skills in one or more of the areas.

Application for Trainees After the Group Meeting

Ask the trainees to write a plan of action to assist in improving these areas that need developing.

EXERCISE 19.8
UNDERSTANDING OTHERS

Goal

To assist trainees in understanding that different learning styles exist in the classroom and that provision for all learning styles needs to be considered

Introduction to the Exercise

Any learning situation depends on the teacher and the learner and the interaction that occurs between the two. The leader needs to make sure that some of the activities in the lesson are designed for different types of learning styles.

Training Procedures

1. Discuss the homework from the previous exercise.
2. Preview the appropriate material from Module XXIII: Peer Helping Through Tutoring.

3. Ask the trainees to complete the "Different Ways To Learn" chart.

4. Have the entire group share the different ways, so that all areas are covered (list on the board).

5. Brainstorm additional ways of teaching different styles of learning.

Application for Trainees After the Group Meeting

1. Ask the trainees to demonstrate activities that show how they would teach a group on "How to Cook Breakfast."

2. Make sure they have a variety of activities that appeal to different types of learning.

EXERCISE 19.9
MOTIVATING OTHERS

Goal

To help trainees understand what motivates them, as well as others, in terms of learning

Introduction to the Exercise

Motivation is very difficult to teach and understand, and trainees will need to recognize this to prevent becoming discouraged as they try to motivate others. Help trainees understand what motivates them, as well as others.

Training Procedures

1. Review the homework from the previous exercise.
2. Lead the group through the "Visualization Exercise."

Visualization Exercise

1. Play soft music in the background.
2. Have each person get very comfortable.

3. Relax each part of the body (take them through each body part). Use a visualizing exercise from a book or use a visualizing tape if you have not previously gained proficiency in this exercise.

4. Imagine a very quiet place that is special (e.g., mountain, ocean).

5. Imagine that you are learning a new task.
    a. What got you excited?
    b. What is happening?
    c. What was the thing that the leader did that helped you to learn?
    d. Open your eyes and feel refreshed and relaxed.

6. Have the participants draw and/or describe in writing the scene in their imagery work.

7. Discuss the image with the entire group.

8. Write the motivator on the board.

9. Get the group to brainstorm examples of a motivator.

Application for Trainees After the Group Meeting

1. Have trainees think of motivating activities for teaching others how to get along with their peers.
2. Have trainees prepare for Exercise 19.10.

EXERCISE 19.10
PUBLIC SPEAKING SKILLS

Goal

To teach trainees specific skills in public speaking

Introduction to the Exercise

This exercise is not meant to be a complete class in speech. It is designed to focus on specific skills needed for speaking to large groups.

Training Procedures

1. Review the homework from the previous exercise.
2. Review the "Public Speaking Skills" listed in *Peer Power, Book Two, Workbook*, as well as others that you think are important.
3. Have the trainees discuss a topic they know well for 5 minutes. They may use notes.
4. Ask the audience to give feedback concerning public speaking skills. They may use the "Public Speaking Skills" list.

Application for Trainees After the Group Meeting

1. Ask trainees to practice in front of a mirror and observe their nonverbal behavior as they talk.
2. Ask trainees to prepare for Exercise 19.11.

EXERCISE 19.11
PLANNING FOR LARGE GROUPS

Goal

To teach trainees some of the skills needed in planning a lesson

Introduction to the Exercise

If a large group lesson goes well, it is generally because the leader is organized and has a lesson plan. The art of planning is difficult. Once you have a plan, it will be much easier to make modifications if things are not going well, rather than if you have no plan at all.

Training Procedures

1. Review the homework from the previous exercise.
2. Review the steps needed for planning a lesson.

3. Have the trainees work in triads to design a classroom presentation on "Good Listening Skills."

4. Work with each of the groups to assist in their thinking and planning.

5. Have someone from each group share their lesson plan with the entire group.

Application for Trainees After the Group Meeting

1. Ask trainees to refine the lesson plan.

2. Ask trainees to prepare for Exercise 19.12.

EXERCISE 19.12
PRACTICE A LARGE CLASSROOM GROUP PRESENTATION

Goal

To provide trainees practice in leading a classroom group with a set lesson

Introduction to the Exercise

To decide how long each activity will take and have all of the materials available is a difficult task. Using the two examples included in this exercise allows each trainee to lead the other trainees in the activity.

Training Procedures

1. Review the homework.

2. Go over the two sample classroom exercises provided in the *Peer Power, Book Two, Workbook* and demonstrate.

3. Divide into groups of four or five participants.

4. Have each person present one of the lessons for the remainder of the group.

5. Have one person play the observer role and give the leader feedback.

Application for Trainees After the Group Meeting

1. Ask trainees to read the introduction to Module XX.
2. Ask trainees to prepare for Exercise 20.1.

MODULE

ENHANCING SEXUAL HEALTH THROUGH PEER HELPING

Goal

To enable trainees to help others address sexual health issues, either one-on-one or in groups

Approximate Time

Module Introduction
Application—10 to 15 minutes

Exercise 20.1—30 to 40 minutes in training session
Application—15 minutes

Exercise 20.2—30 to 60 minutes in training session
Application—20 minutes

Exercise 20.3—30 to 60 minutes in training session

Exercise 20.4—60 to 90 minutes in training session
Application—15 minutes

Exercise 20.5—30 to 60 minutes in training session

Exercise 20.6—60 to 90 minutes in training session

Application—15 minutes

Materials

- *Peer Power, Book Two, Workbook* (one copy for each trainee)
- Optional: It is highly recommended that you bring in your health teacher or someone from the county health department to present lessons on STDs and HIV/AIDS. Be sure to identify local statistics and local referral sources, along with their addresses and phone numbers.

Introduction to the Module

Enhancing sexual health is an important role for peer helpers. Often, peers can be effective in preventing the spread of HIV/AIDS and STDs. They are also vital in getting help for those who may have sexual issues. This module may not be appropriate for your peer helping group to take on as a tool to help others. Peer helpers can use the information to educate themselves and to help others. If you use this with high school students, you may want written permission from the parents of the youth who are serving as peer helpers, as well as the target group. Since this has become a critical health issue with youth, information on how to manage sexual health is imperative. It is also important to teach alternative actions and decision making that pertains to sexual activities.

Training Procedures

1. Determine the exercises to use for this module.
2. Decide if it is desirable to use your local statistics for the examples discussed.
3. Be aware that the local statistics may cause problems with the trainees in the session.
4. This module could be used along with Module XIX: Group Work.
5. You may want to include information obtained from your local health department to add to the material listed in this module.

6. After the peer helpers are trained in facilitating groups, design projects to use in small groups or one-on-one helping.

Evaluation Process

Evaluate the process used in the teaching of this module through the feedback obtained from the participants, as well as by their written work and evaluation materials.

You may want to use J.10 from the CD included with *Peer Programs*.

Measuring Outcomes

1. Use Exercise 20.1 to determine knowledge about HIV/AIDS and STDs.
2. Use Exercise 20.2 to assess additional knowledge about HIV/AIDS and Exercise 20.3 for additional knowledge about STDs.
3. Use Exercise 20.6 to measure skills in the decision-making (problem-solving) areas of sexual health.

EXERCISE 20.1
HOW MUCH DO YOU KNOW ABOUT HIV/AIDS AND STDs?

Goals

To help trainees learn about HIV/AIDS and STDs

To help trainees consider the decision-making process concerning sexual health

Introduction to the Exercise

This is a questionnaire that can be given to the trainees to determine their knowledge regarding sex-related diseases. It is good to discuss the answers to the questionnaire.

Training Procedures

1. Ask the trainees to answer the questions, either prior to the training session or during the session.
2. Review the answers to the questionnaire with the entire group. You may want to give the questionnaire again at the end of the module.
3. Give a prize to the person who has the most correct answers.
4. You may want to assign the trainees to read about and do reports on a variety of topics concerning sexual health.

Answers to the Questionnaire:

1. False—AIDS is the end of HIV infection and may not appear for more than 10 years after infection.
2. False—A person can be infected with HIV and capable of transmitting it to others for up to 10 years or longer before having any outward symptoms.
3. False—Teens, like anyone else, can get HIV. Many teens have HIV but have no symptoms, and they may not even be aware they have the virus.
4. True—These are the safer sexual behaviors that allow partners to give each other pleasure, short of engaging in sexual intercourse.
5. True—Gonorrhea and especially herpes cause sores that can provide an easy entry for HIV, the virus that causes AIDS.
6. True—Sharing needles has become a major way to transmit HIV. The blood on the needle, not the drug or steroid, is the way HIV is spread.
7. False—Symptoms of viral STDs, such as herpes and genital warts, can be controlled through medication, but cannot be cured. Many bacterial STDs, such as chlamydia and gonorrhea, are not life-threatening, but may cause extensive internal damage and discomfort, if not diagnosed and treated. (Try to get the most current information from the Health Department or CDC.)

8. False—Steroids cause other problems, but not HIV or AIDS. It makes no difference what substance is injected. If there is HIV-infected blood on the needle, it can transmit HIV, and may cause AIDS.

9. True—While not 100% effective because of breakage and leakage, latex condoms are the best forms of protection from sexually transmitted diseases.

10. False—AIDS is a disease caused by HIV, a virus. Anyone—homosexual or heterosexual, male or female—can get HIV.

11. False—There is much research to develop a vaccine to prevent HIV and to prevent AIDS from developing in people who already have HIV; however, no vaccine is available yet.

12. True—There is often a long latency period between infection and first symptoms; it is thought that most of the people in the United States who have HIV are unaware of their condition.

13. False—Blood donation is completely safe; the needle used to draw the blood is sterile and is used only once, then discarded so no infectious diseases can be transmitted in this way.

14. False—"AIDS test" is a misnomer. There is no such test. A standard blood test for antibodies indicates HIV, the virus that causes AIDS, and will tell if a person has HIV in their blood.

15. False—Because there is a big "if"! Sex is safe only if neither partner is infected, and that's virtually impossible to know without a special blood test.

16. False—Birth-control pills are almost 100% effective in preventing pregnancy, but they offer no protection against STDs.

17. False—Even if you know your partner well, you cannot know about the health status of his or her previous sexual partners.

18. True—Drinking alcohol lowers the ability to make good decisions. A person who is drunk may engage in risky behaviors that he or she would not do otherwise.

19. True—The only 100% safe behavior is abstinence. Those who are sexually active will substantially reduce the risk of infection through the use of a latex condom. The use of injection drugs puts one at risk when the needle is shared.

20. False—The term "sexual intercourse" refers to vaginal, anal, or oral intercourse.

21. True—Genital HPV cannot be entirely prevented by condom use.

Application for Trainees After the Group Meeting

1. Have the trainees review information on the Internet or other sources pertaining to sexual health.
2. Ask trainees to prepare for Exercise 20.2.

EXERCISE 20.2
HIV/AIDS

Goal

To help trainees learn about HIV/AIDS

Introduction to the Exercise

HIV/AIDS has become a pandemic worldwide and needs to be viewed as a major public health issue. It is always helpful to get local statistics, if available.

Training Procedures

1. Review the information on HIV/AIDS.
2. Ask the trainees to write the answers to the last two questions.
3. Ask the trainees to discuss the answers with the training group.

Applications for Trainees After the Group Meeting

1. Ask trainees to read Exercise 20.3.
2. Ask trainees to describe in writing how they feel about Exercise 20.2.

EXERCISE 20.3
STDs

Goal

To provide the trainees with information about STDs

Introduction to the Exercise

STDs have become a big problem with today's youth, because of lack of information and embarrassment. Give the peer helpers information to assist others in learning about STDs.

Training Procedures

1. Ask for feedback regarding the application for Exercise 20.2.
2. Review the STD warning signs and treatment. It is helpful to have a health teacher, physician, or health department representative available to discuss this issue.
3. Discuss how to inform others.
4. Discuss how to reduce the stigma of getting help with the group.
5. Work in groups of four to design informative messages about STDs.
6. Present these messages to the entire group.

Application for Trainees After the Group Meeting

1. Ask trainees to look over Exercise 20.4.
2. Ask trainees to present the messages to a target population.

EXERCISE 20.4
LEARNING THE LANGUAGE
OF STDs, HIV, AND AIDS

Goal

To have the trainees learn the expressions used in sexual health language

Introduction to the Exercise

The expressions used in sexual health language are vital to be able to communicate with others.

Training Procedures

1. Review the terms in Exercise 20.4.
2. Ask trainees to work in teams of four to answer questions in the student workbook.
3. Give 10 points for each correct answer.
4. Keep track of the points for each team.
5. Give a prize to the team with the most points.

Application for Trainees After the Group Meeting

1. Have trainees refer back to the questions in Exercise 20.1, to see how they understand the information.
2. Ask trainees to prepare for Exercise 20.5.

EXERCISE 20.5
REDUCING RISKY BEHAVIOR THROUGH
SEXUAL RESPONSIBILITY

Goal

To help the trainees identify risky behaviors and increase personal sexual responsibility

Introduction to the Exercise

This exercise will help trainees understand risky behavior and personal sexual responsibility.

Training Procedures

1. Ask the trainees to work in groups of four.
2. Write each activity on large index cards. Trainees can add additional activities.
3. Have each group rank-order the cards, from the least risky behavior to the most risky. Ask trainees to come to a group consensus. Help them identify the rationale for their rankings.
4. Ask them to discuss ways to help others with HIV/AIDS or STDs.
5. Ask an outside speaker to come in to discuss the rankings.

Application for Trainees After the Group Meeting

1. Ask trainees to look over Exercise 20.6.
2. Have trainees write a reaction to Exercise 20.5.

EXERCISE 20.6
DECISION MAKING

Goal

To help the trainees gain experience in decision making, communication, and refusal skills

Introduction to the Exercise

This can be a lot of fun and will lead to discussion. You may also want to have trainees write their own stories or endings to the current story.

Training Procedures

1. Ask for feedback from Exercise 20.5.
2. Review the decision-making steps.
3. Read the story (or have a peer read the story) out loud.
4. Discuss the questions under number 4 in the student workbook.
5. Divide the training group into two teams and have them play the Decision Game.
6. Allow them 15 minutes to play the Decision Game. The team that has the most decisions wins.
7. Ask trainees to discuss the rationale for their decisions.

Application for Trainees After the Group Meeting

1. Ask trainees to look over Exercise 20.1.
2. Ask trainees to prepare for Exercise 20.1.
3. You may want to use reflection questions from J.10 in the CD in the *Peer Programs* book.

MODULE **XXI**

RECOGNIZING DISORDERED EATING PROBLEMS

Goals

To teach trainees about disordered eating

To help trainees become aware of their potential for developing disordered eating

To teach trainees signs of disordered eating in others

To teach trainees some intervention techniques for dealing with people who have disordered eating

Approximate Time

Module Introduction—30 minutes for application review

Exercise 21.1—30 to 60 minutes in training session

Application—30 minutes

Exercise 21.2—30 to 60 minutes in training session

Application—30 minutes

Exercise 21.3—60 minutes in training session

Application—30 minutes

Exercise 21.4—30 to 60 minutes in training session

Application—30 minutes

Exercise 21.5—60 to 120 minutes in training session

Application—30 minutes

Exercise 21.6—60 minutes in training session

Application—20 minutes

Exercise 21.7—60 minutes in training session

Application—15 minutes

Exercise 21.8—60 minutes in training session

Application—15 minutes

Materials

- Optional: DVD or CD on disordered eating
- Optional: Obtain and distribute pamphlets from some of the references.
- Speaker: Ask someone from disordered eating programs or from Overeaters Anonymous to come and talk with the group.

Introduction to the Module

Disordered eating is on the rise in this country. Anorexia, bulimia, and compulsive overeating are dangerous illnesses that often need intervention. Disordered eating is a progressive, addictive disease in which the behavior becomes very compulsive and generally gets worse before getting better. Multiple interventions are needed for individuals suffering from disordered eating. Sometimes, hospitalization and outpatient help are also required. Generally, the involvement of a dietitian, psychiatrist, medical doctor, dentist, and psychologist are needed in the treatment. This module, along with Module XV: Taking Care of You! Stress Management, can be taught together. Help the trainees understand they should refer those with disordered eating to a professional mental health person if they encounter this problem rather than deal with the problem personally. Exercises from the module can be used in the classroom presentations and/or small group discussions.

Training Procedures

1. Determine the number of training sessions and exercises to be included in this module.
2. Review the content to be covered, as well as the suggested activities, as listed in *Peer Power, Book Two, Workbook*.
3. Be prepared to practice or show a video of a person with disordered eating.
4. You may want to schedule a speaker on disordered eating early in the training.
5. It will be helpful to have the peer helpers order materials from the resources listed at the end of Exercise 21.7.
6. Ask the peer helpers to keep a journal of their food intake and complete their application assignments.

Evaluation Process

You can evaluate the process used in teaching this module through trainee feedback, by observation of their written work, and by trainee behavior when practicing the skills during training sessions.

Measuring Outcomes

1. Use Exercise 21.1 to allow trainees to assess their own disordered eating.
2. Use Exercise 21.3 to enable trainees to judge their own potential disordered eating. They should also consider their responsibility as an enabler of someone else with disordered eating.
3. Watch and listen closely to the trainees during the practice session in Exercise 21.6 to determine trainees are at ease using the techniques learned earlier in the module, along

with skills of empathy and confrontation. You may want to have the trainees tape their practice sessions, and use the tapes during your evaluation process.

4. You may want to use J.10 from the CD in *Peer Programs*.

EXERCISE 21.1
FOOD CHART

Goals

To provide the trainees with an opportunity to keep a food chart

To review the introductory material

Introduction to the Exercise

This module will help trainees learn some facts about disordered eating. It would benefit the trainees to view a DVD or listen to a lecture on the topic. In this exercise the trainees will get in touch with their own eating patterns.

1. Review the material from the introduction, as well as the reaction of the trainees to films or speakers.
2. Discuss the material to determine if the trainees agree with it.
3. Have the trainees keep a food chart for a week.
4. Have trainees chart their food from yesterday, and walk them through the chart.
5. Ask trainees how they would like to change their eating behavior.

Application for Trainees After the Group Meeting

1. Ask the trainees to keep a journal of their application assignments during the entire module.
2. Ask trainees to keep a "Food Intake Chart" and bring it in each training session.
3. Have trainees prepare for Exercise 21.2.

EXERCISE 21.2
ASSESSING DISORDERED EATING

Goals

To allow trainees to examine their own risk for disordered eating

To teach trainees how to recognize disordered eating problems in others

Introduction to the Exercise

As individuals become aware of their own disordered eating risk, many will begin to seek professional help to reduce the problem. As peer helpers recognize these risk factors in others, they will need to refer them to mental health professionals. Often peer helpers are the first to recognize eating problems. Hopefully, they would refer the person with the problem to seek professional help.

Training Procedures

1. Discuss the trainees' homework from the previous exercise, and review the goals they have set.
2. Have the trainees answer "yes" or "no" to the "Self-Assessment Checklist on Disordered Eating."
3. Ask the trainees to share information from the checklist with the group.
4. Have group members assist each other in suggesting intervention strategies to reduce eating problems.
5. Ask trainees to think of someone they know and try to assess the person's potential for developing disordered eating.

Application for Trainees After the Group Meeting

1. Have trainees continue with their journal.
2. Ask the trainees to write their reactions to their eating behavior in the journal.
3. Have trainees prepare for Exercise 21.3.

EXERCISE 21.3
BULIMIA, ANOREXIA, COMPULSIVE OVEREATING: WHERE ARE YOU AS A DISORDERED EATING PERSON OR ENABLER?

Goals

To help trainees understand that disordered eating is a progressive disorder

To help trainees understand the concept of codependency in disordered eating

Introduction to the Exercise

Disordered eating is a progressive, addictive disease. Unlike alcoholism or chemical dependency, one cannot stop eating. Therefore, it is important to examine the level the individual is at on the disease chart ratings. It is also important to look at the issue of codependency to determine if the person with disordered eating is also codependent to someone else.

Training Procedures

1. Review and discuss the application journal and food chart from the two previous exercises.
2. Review the two charts in *Peer Power, Book Two, Workbook.*
3. Review the characteristics of codependency. If conducted within the group, tact must be utilized because of the effect upon those trainees who are codependent or who have a relationship with someone who is.
4. Discuss ways to get out of the codependency.

Application for Trainees After the Group Meeting

1. Ask trainees to continue keeping their food charts and journals.
2. Ask trainees to focus on items in Directions 2 through 5.

EXERCISE 21.4
FOOD CHOICE EVALUATION

Goals

To review the four food groups

To determine if the trainees are eating food from each of the four food groups

Introduction to the Exercise

It is important to know the four food groups in order to use that knowledge as a guide to healthy eating. It would be beneficial to have a dietitian speak to the group before this activity.

Training Procedures

1. Review the application from the previous exercise.
2. Ask the trainees to bring in their food charts for use during the last full day of training.
3. Record information from the food chart to the "Food Record," and follow the directions for the food choice evaluation. Review U.S. Dietary Goals.
4. Review the "Food Selection Changes" and help trainees set goals for healthy eating.

Application for Trainees After the Group Meeting

1. Have trainees do their application based on questions from the book and continue work with the food charts.
2. Have trainees prepare for Exercise 21.5.

EXERCISE 21.5
CULTURAL IMPACT OF DISORDERED EATING

Goals

To help trainees understand the cultural impact of eating problems

To help trainees understand self-worth and body image

Introduction to the Exercise

Men and women are influenced by the media (TV, magazines, billboards, etc.). Media plays a role in disordered eating.

Training Procedures

1. Review the application work.
2. Allow plenty of time for this activity, and utilize popular magazines for both men and women.
3. Ask the trainees to observe billboards and TV commercials.
4. As they are looking at pictures in the magazines, point out certain pictures that make the point of the difference between media and real-world individuals at work, supermarkets, and in real situations.
5. Have a discussion regarding the cultural expectation for thinness and fitness, and how this affects individuals' self-esteem.
6. Have trainees work at an art table, cutting out pictures and applying them to poster boards. Make sure you have enough poster board and glue for everyone.
7. Have trainees make a collage to describe themselves.
8. Ask each person to present their collage to the rest of the group and explain their collage.
9. At the end of the session, discuss how much emphasis is placed on beauty, body size, etc.

Application for Trainees After the Group Meeting

1. Ask trainees to turn in an essay at the next training session concerning their view of the impact of culture on eating behaviors.
2. Ask trainees to react to the collage. Would they like to be different than they presently are?

EXERCISE 21.6
BODY IMAGE AND THE IMPACT ON DISORDERED EATING

Goal

To raise awareness regarding the impact body image has on disordered eating

Introduction to the Exercise

You may want to review some of the issues that impact body image such as the media, messages we hear from family, friends, coaches, and so on.

Training Procedures

1. Review some of the basic issues that impact body image.
2. Facilitate a group discussion regarding how these issues impact on body image.

Application for Trainees After the Group Meeting

1. Ask trainees to write the reaction to the exercise.
2. Ask trainees to read over Exercise 21.7

EXERCISE 21.7
PRACTICE IN HELPING A PERSON WITH DISORDERED EATING

Goals

To help trainees learn intervention techniques for coping with another person who has disordered eating

To help trainees learn when they must refer to a mental health professional(s)

Introduction to the Exercise

It is important to stress that disordered eating is too serious an issue for peer helpers to deal with by themselves. They will need additional help if they are dealing with a disordered eating candidate.

Training Procedures

1. Review and discuss the homework journal from the previous Exercises 21.5 and 21.6.
2. Review materials learned earlier.
3. Review skills of attending, empathy, questioning, and confrontation.
4. Review observer role.
5. Demonstrate practice of "helping first."
6. Ask participants to work together in groups of three.
7. Move from group to group to assess helpers.

Application for Trainees After the Group Meeting

1. Ask trainees to continue writing in their journal.
2. Assign outside reading, if available.
3. Have the peer helpers get local information concerning help for disordered eating or use the Internet.
4. Ask trainees to prepare for Exercise 21.8.

EXERCISE 21.8
LOOKING AT MYSELF

Goals

To examine how the individual trainees view themselves in relation to all the material they have learned and have been writing about

To help trainees set goals for the future

Introduction to the Exercise

In this exercise, we can review all the previous lessons as well as talk about eating disorders being multidimensional.

Training Procedures

1. Have the trainees complete Direction 1 and help them discuss each one with you and participants.
2. Assist trainees to set new goals relative to their eating behavior and exercise behavior.
3. Have the trainees share their goals with the group.
4. Collect the journals and respond to the writing of the trainees.
5. Use the journal for evaluation.

Application for Trainees After the Group Meeting

1. Ask trainees to read the information in the first part of Module XXII.
2. Ask trainees to prepare for Exercise 22.1.

MODULE

SUICIDE PREVENTION

Goals

To teach trainees about suicide

To assist trainees in becoming aware of their own potential for suicide

To teach trainees the warning signs of potential suicide in others

To teach trainees intervention techniques for those who may be considering suicide

Approximate Time

Module Introduction

Application—10 to 15 minutes

Explaining the issues—30 to 40 minutes in training session

Exercise 22.1—30 to 60 minutes in training session

Application—30 to 60 minutes

Exercise 22.2—30 to 60 minutes in training session

Application—30 to 60 minutes

Exercise 22.3—30 to 60 minutes in training session

Application—20 minutes

Exercise 22.4—60 to 90 minutes in training session

Application—10 minutes

Exercise 22.5—60 minutes in training session

Application—30 to 60 minutes

Materials

- *Peer Power, Book Two, Workbook* (one for each trainee)
- Optional: Show a DVD or CD on suicide prevention.
- Optional: Obtain and distribute pamphlets from some of the suicide prevention organizations.
- Speaker: Arrange for a speaker from a hospice unit or a suicide prevention center.

Introduction to the Module

Suicide was an epidemic in the 1990s and continues to be prevalent in this decade as well. Most of us know someone who has committed or attempted suicide. Suicide has become an alternative to deal with stress. Many persons have a difficult time coping with stress in a healthy manner. Peer helpers need to understand clearly that, rather than try to handle a potential suicide situation, they should refer the individual to a mental health professional. This module might be taught along with Module XV: Taking Care of You! Stress Management.

Speakers may be used with this module.

Training Procedures

1. Determine the number of training sessions and exercises to be included in this module.
2. Review the content to be covered, as well as the suggested activities listed in *Peer Power, Book Two, Workbook*.
3. Present a model practice or videotape that shows how to help a suicidal person.

4. If a speaker is to be used, you may want to schedule the speaker early in the training session.

5. Request that peer helpers order material from the resources listed.

Evaluation Process

You can evaluate the process used in teaching a skill through the trainee feedback, and by observation of their written work, as well as their behavior when practicing the skills during training sessions.

Measuring Outcomes

1. Use Exercise 22.1 to help trainees find their own stress level.

2. Use Exercise 22.2 to enable trainees to judge their own vulnerability to suicide.

3. Watch and listen closely during the practice in Exercise 22.5 to gauge the ease with which trainees use the techniques of intervention learned in Exercise 22.3.

EXERCISE 22.1
STRESS SELF-EVALUATION

Goals

To provide trainees an opportunity to assess their own stress level

To review introductory material

Introduction to the Exercise

This module will assist trainees in learning facts about suicide. It would be beneficial to show a film related to suicide at this time. The trainees will also learn to recognize their own level of stress.

Training Procedures

1. Review material from the introduction, as well as the reaction of the trainees to the film.
2. Discuss the material to determine if the trainees agree with it.
3. Have the trainees take "The Teen Scene: Stress Test."
4. Discuss their results and what these results mean to the trainees.
5. Use brainstorming techniques for reducing stress in the lives of the trainees.
6. Ask trainees to set goals to help them deal with stress.

Application for Trainees After the Group Meeting

1. Ask the trainees to keep a journal during this module regarding their feelings and reactions to the discussion on suicide.
2. Ask trainees to specifically focus on a plan to deal with their own stress level, based on their score from "The Teen Scene: Stress Test."
3. Ask trainees to write some goal(s) to deal with stress in their lives.

EXERCISE 22.2
SUICIDE RISKS

Goals

To provide an opportunity for trainees to examine their own risk for suicide

To teach trainees how to recognize suicide risk in others

Introduction to the Exercise

As individuals become aware of their own suicide risk, many will begin to seek professional help to reduce the risk.

As peer helpers recognize these risk factors in others, they should refer them to mental health professionals. It has been found that once peer helpers are trained to recognize these risk factors, referrals to mental health professionals increase as they see more serious issues.

Training Procedures

1. Discuss their application from the previous exercise, and review the goals decided upon by the trainees.
2. Have trainees review the list of possible suicide risk factors.
3. Ask trainees to share their score with the group.
4. Have trainees assist each other in suggesting intervention strategies to reduce risk factors.
5. Ask trainees to think of someone they know and assess their potential for suicide.

Application for Trainees After the Group Meeting

1. Have the trainees continue writing in their journal.
2. Ask the trainees to formulate a written plan to reduce their own potential for suicide.
3. Ask trainees to think of someone they know who exhibits several of the risk factors and plan an intervention to encourage them to seek professional help.
4. Prepare for Exercise 22.3.

EXERCISE 22.3
INTERVENTION TECHNIQUES

Goals

To help trainees learn intervention techniques for coping with a potential suicide candidate

To help trainees learn that they must refer potential suicide candidates to mental health professionals for help

Introduction to the Exercise

It is imperative that you stress the consequences of suicide intervention to the peer helpers. Trainees must seek additional help if the person with whom they are dealing is a suicide candidate.

Training Procedures

1. Review and discuss the journal writing from the previous exercise.
2. Review intervention techniques, discuss them with the group, and help participants explore additional techniques.
3. Identify those techniques the trainees agree and disagree with.
4. Brainstorm a plan of action in dealing with a potentially suicidal person with the entire group.
5. Have trainees develop a resource list of local mental health professionals and materials for use in working with suicidal persons and/or those affected by a suicide.

Application for Trainees After the Group Meeting

1. Have the trainees continue writing in their journal.
2. Assign outside reading if available.
3. Ask trainess to prepare for Exercise 22.4.

EXERCISE 22.4
ASSISTING THOSE LEFT TO LIVE
ON AFTER A SUICIDE

Goals

To assist trainees in understanding the impact of suicide on others

To assist trainees in setting up a plan to assist survivors

Introduction to the Exercise

This is a good exercise to utilize a speaker, perhaps from a hospice or suicide prevention group. The issue of dealing with loss, using Kübler-Ross material that deals with grieving, is very appropriate for this exercise. Depending on the population served by the peer helpers (e.g., school, hospital, business), they may wish to develop a plan to deal with suicide, should it happen.

Training Procedures

1. Review the journal from the previous exercise.
2. Review "Stages of Loss"; show a film if appropriate or have a speaker.
3. Discuss ways the peer helper can assist a survivor.
4. Discuss how a local community can develop a plan to utilize peer helpers to assist survivors when a suicide occurs.

Application for Trainees After the Group Meeting

1. Have trainees write how they might react to helping a survivor of suicide.
2. Have trainees describe in writing what their thoughts and feelings would be if they were to lose someone close to them to suicide.
3. Ask trainees to prepare for Exercise 22.5.

EXERCISE 22.5
PRACTICE IN HELPING A SUICIDAL PERSON

Goals

To help trainees practice how to work with a suicidal person

To help trainees practice getting the potential helpee to seek out a mental health professional

Introduction to the Exercise

Peer helpers are often put in the position of recognizing that someone is considering suicide. Sometimes they try to handle it themselves. This exercise will help trainees learn the skills required to persuade an individual to seek professional help. Each practice round may last 20 to 30 minutes. Trainees should practice their basic skills (e.g., attending, empathy, questioning) and advanced intervention techniques. They may want to use situations they have created for practice.

Training Procedures

1. Demonstrate the following practice session. Use information from the previous exercises; demonstrate using the introduction material, and the skills from *Peer Power, Book One*.

    Example: Potential suicide victims: The potential victim is a white male, an excellent student, and a perfectionist. The boy slashed his wrist earlier this year when a good friend was killed in a car accident. He has few friends, and recently has been very depressed. To deal with his depression, he has started drinking on the weekends.

2. Divide the class into groups of three, and practice being a potential suicide victim, a helper, and an observer. Change roles until all have had a chance to play all three roles.

3. The observer should use the forms in the exercises containing guides for the observer.

4. Discuss the trainees' reactions to all roles.

Application for Trainees After the Group Meeting

1. Ask the trainees to describe their feelings about the activity in their journal.

2. Ask the trainees to request information from referral sources (list developed in Exercise 22.3).

3. Ask trainees to turn in their journals following this exercise.

4. Ask trainees to prepare for Module XXIII and Exercise 23.1.

MODULE

COPING WITH LOSS

Goals

To teach trainees about loss

To help trainees understand how to deal with loss

To help trainees to understand grieving

To allow trainees to practice helping others cope with loss

Approximate Time

Module Introduction—10 minutes

Exercise 23.1—60 minutes in training session
Application—30 minutes

Exercise 23.2—60 minutes in training session
Application—30 minutes

Exercise 23.3—60 minutes in training session
Application—30 minutes

Exercise 23.4—60 to 90 minutes in training session
Application—30 minutes

Materials

- *Peer Power, Book Two, Workbook* (one copy for each trainee)
- Optional: Show DVD or CD on death and dying.
- Speaker: Arrange for a representative from a hospice unit to speak to the group.

Introduction to the Module

This module can be very emotional for the group members. A high level of trust and skills is needed when you teach this module. You may need to spend additional time on this module.

Training Procedures

1. Determine the number of training sessions and exercises to be included in this module.
2. Review the content to be covered and the suggested activities as listed in *Peer Power, Book Two, Workbook*.
3. Be prepared to share your own loss and how you coped with it.
4. An expert speaker would be beneficial to the session.

Evaluation Process

You can evaluate the process used in teaching these skills by the trainee feedback, by observation of their written work, and by their behavior when practicing a skill.

Measuring Outcomes

1. Use Exercise 23.4 to review skills.
2. Use written homework.

EXERCISE 23.1
MY OWN LOSSES

Goal

To have trainees look at personal loss and how to cope with it

Introduction to the Exercise

This exercise can be very powerful. It is important that time is allowed for the exercise, as well as sufficient discussion opportunity.

Training Procedures

1. Discuss loss line with trainees.
2. Show trainees an example.
3. Have trainees draw "My Age-Loss Line." Use newsprint or poster board, if results are to be shared with the group.
4. Ask trainees to share their loss line within a small group or with the entire group.
5. Discuss how they coped.
6. Point out the impact if too many losses occur too close together.

Application for Trainees After the Group Meeting

1. Have trainees describe in writing their reaction to the exercise.
2. Have trainees prepare for Exercise 23.2.

EXERCISE 23.2
TYPES OF LOSS

Goal

To help trainees learn the types of loss they have encountered and how they coped

Introduction to the Exercise

We all have dealt with loss at some point in our lives. How did we cope with it? Did formal rituals help?

Training Procedures

1. Discuss the exercise and have trainees list their losses. Identify ways of coping.
2. This is a good exercise in which to show a loss-related film or have a guest speaker who deals with rituals of loss—formal (funerals) and informal (talking).
3. Explain rituals, both formal and informal rituals, and give examples of each.
4. Discuss the activity with the entire group.

Application for Trainees After the Group Meeting

1. Have trainees describe in a journal a reaction to this exercise, with an emphasis on coping.
2. Have trainees prepare for Exercise 23.3.

EXERCISE 23.3
THE GRIEVING PROCESS

Goal

To help trainees understand the grieving process

Introduction to the Exercise

In this exercise, trainees will learn the grieving process, and how to reference their own level of grieving.

Training Procedures

1. Review the grieving process.
2. Lead a discussion to determine the level where each person is in the grieving process.
3. Explore the different grief feelings individuals have at the different stages.
4. Have a discussion on how this knowledge will benefit trainees when working with others.

Application for Trainees After the Group Meeting

1. Have trainees record in their journal their reaction to the grieving process.
2. Have trainees prepare for Exercise 23.4.

EXERCISE 23.4
OFFERING SUPPORT TO OTHERS

Goal

To provide for trainees practice in helping individuals cope with the loss process

Introduction to the Exercise

Often individuals are uncomfortable talking about loss. This exercise will help the trainees listen to others and discuss their loss.

Training Procedures

1. Review "The Grieving Process" in Exercise 23.3.
2. Supply trainees with referral sources. Have trainees add to and modify the list from Exercise 22.3.

3. Divide the training group into triads and appoint one helper, one helpee, and one observer. Ask them to discuss a personal example of a loss.

4. Have the observer give feedback, and have trainees play each role.

Application for Trainees After the Group Meeting

1. Have trainees write their concepts about their role as support to someone who is experiencing grief.

2. Have trainees prepare for Module XXIV and Exercise 24.1.

MODULE

HIGHWAY TRAFFIC SAFETY

Goal

To teach trainees about the issues of highway traffic safety

Approximate Time

Module Introduction—10 minutes

Exercise 24.1—60 to 90 minutes in training session
Application—30 to 60 minutes

Exercise 24.2—30 to 60 minutes in training session
Application—15 minutes

Exercise 24.3—30 to 60 minutes in training session
Application—60 minutes

Exercise 24.4—60 to 90 minutes in training session
Application—30 minutes

Exercise 24.5—30 to 60 minutes in training session
Application—30 minutes

Materials

- *Peer Power, Book Two, Workbook* (one copy for each trainee)
- Optional: Show DVD or CD on highway traffic safety. *SMASHED* is a good free HBO DVD that can be ordered from http://www.noys.org.
- Speaker: Secure a speaker from your state's Department of Transportation or local police.

Introduction to the Module

This module is a vital component of any peer-led program. Highway traffic safety is important for any age group. An obvious safety issue is substance abuse while driving. Other issues, including distracted driving and failure to use seat belts are critical issues to address in teaching traffic safety. Be sensitive to special issues pertaining to traffic safety when working with Hispanics, African Americans, and Asians.

Training Procedures

1. Determine the number of training sessions and exercises to be included in this module.
2. Review the content to be covered, and the suggested activities as listed in *Peer Power, Book Two, Workbook*.
3. If you show *SMASHED*, you can download the training guide from http://www.noys.org.
4. Speakers from the Department of Transportation, local police, or Mothers Against Drunk Driving are good resources to utilize.

Evaluation Process

You can evaluate the process used in teaching highway traffic safety skills by trainee feedback, and by observation of their written work and behavior when practicing a presentation. During this module, try to get the peer helpers to sign a pledge card concerning substance abuse and driving, distracted driving, and seat belt use.

Measuring Outcomes

1. Use Exercise 24.1 to review trainees' presentations.
2. Use written material from the trainees to evaluate their integration of facts and attitudes and behavior.

EXERCISE 24.1
THE FACTS OF HIGHWAY TRAFFIC SAFETY

Goals

To teach the facts pertaining to highway traffic safety

To have trainees prepare an interactive lesson to present the facts to their peers

Introduction to the Exercise

You may want to show the DVD *SMASHED* during this lesson. The most critical portion of this exercise is that the trainees will learn the facts and be able to put together an interactive lesson to share with the other trainees. It may be beneficial to include some of the main points in a PowerPoint presentation.

Training Procedures

1. Review the facts for highway traffic safety. A speaker from the local police department can add local facts.
2. Have trainees work in groups of four to develop an interactive safety lesson. Encourage trainees to use either peer theater, a game show format, or a discussion to keep the activity interactive.

Application for Trainees After the Group Meeting

1. Have trainees write down their reaction to Exercise 24.1.
2. Have trainees prepare for Exercise 24.2.

EXERCISE 24.2
YOUTH RISK FACTORS: HIGHWAY TRAFFIC SAFETY

Goal

To facilitate a lesson that identifies risk factors in youth related to highway traffic safety

Introduction to the Exercise

Research indicates graduated licensing is effective in reducing the number of crashes with youth. Reviewing the risk factors and allowing trainees to identify their own risk factors is helpful.

Training Procedures

1. Review youth risk factors in highway traffic safety.
2. Discuss additional risk factors.
3. Have each trainee share information about others who have been at risk for traffic safety.

Application for Trainees After the Group Meeting

1. Have trainees describe in a journal their reactions to this exercise, emphasizing risk factors and how the facts apply to them.
2. Have trainees prepare for Exercise 24.3.

EXERCISE 24.3
COUNTERMEASURES FOR HIGHWAY TRAFFIC SAFETY

Goal

To train the peer helpers in understanding a variety of countermeasures to help teens drive safely

Introduction to the Exercise

There are a variety of resources peer helpers can review concerning some of the latest strategies to promote youth traffic safety. Suggest trainees review the current legislation in the state concerning youth traffic safety.

Training Procedures

1. Review the promising strategies.
2. Ask trainees to research legislation in the state.
3. Divide trainees into groups to review some of the latest strategies on highway traffic safety for youth.

Application for Trainees After the Group Meeting

1. Have trainees describe in their journal their reaction to this exercise.
2. Have trainees prepare for Exercise 24.4.

EXERCISE 24.4
SOCIAL NORMS APPROACH

Goal

To practice utilizing a positive social norms approach

Introduction to the Exercise

Using a positive social norms approach is an important element in convincing youth to wear seat belts, not use drugs, and not become distracted while driving.

Training Procedures

1. Review the introduction to Exercise 24.4.
2. Ask the group to pick a topic that is important to them, such as seat belt use, not drinking and driving, loud music in the car, cell phone use while driving, etc.

3. Have trainees develop a questionnaire to give to others concerning the topic. Trainees may want to ask the psychology teacher to review the questionnaire. Make the questionnaire very short.
4. Have trainees survey their youth population, either via the Internet or by using paper-and-pencil surveys distributed through homerooms or advisory periods.
5. Have them summarize the results and compile the information in a comprehensible format.
6. Have trainees make a plan to publicize the results through posters, announcements, skits, or blogs.
7. Have them conduct a follow-up survey on the same topic to see if the results change.

Application for Trainees After the Group Meeting

1. Have trainees write about their reaction to the positive social norms approach concerning youth highway traffic safety.
2. Have trainees prepare for Exercise 24.5.

EXERCISE 24.5
STRATEGIES FOR IMPACTING OTHERS TO DRIVE SAFELY

Goal

To practice convincing others to drive safely

Introduction to the Exercise

Once the peer helpers have learned lessons on highway traffic safety, it is important to lead small and large groups in learning about the topic, and persuading participants to sign a commitment form.

Training Procedures

1. Review the introduction to Exercise 24.5.
2. Work with your training group to design a plan to teach others about highway traffic safety, and to sign a commitment plan.
3. Utilize the local police or a school resource officer to help plan the event(s).
4. In order to change behavior of others, it generally takes at least three interactive presentations.
5. Consider having a parent night and making a presentation about youth traffic safety.
6. Give trainees feedback about their presentations.
7. Summarize the number of commitment cards that were signed, and share that information with your administrator and the news media.
8. Your group may want to participate in contests sponsored by National Organizations for Youth Safety (NOYS) (http://www.noys.org) during May, which is Youth Traffic Safety Month.
9. Use observation forms from the module related to group work.

Application for Trainees After the Group Meeting

1. Have trainees write about their reaction to the lessons they presented to others.
2. Have trainees prepare for Module XXV. Read the introduction.

MODULE XXV

BULLYING REDUCTION

Goal

To teach trainees about bullying and strategies to reduce bullying

Approximate Time

Module Introduction—10 minutes

Exercise 25.1—30 to 60 minutes in training session

Application—15 to 30 minutes

Exercise 25.2—30 to 60 minutes in training session

Application—15 minutes

Exercise 25.3—30 to 60 minutes in training session

Application—30 minutes

Materials

- *Peer Power, Book Two, Workbook* (one copy for each trainee)
- Optional: Show a DVD or CD on bullying. A good source of material related to bullying can be found at http://www.stopbullyingnow.hrsa.gov.
- Speaker: Secure a speaker from the Safe and Drug Free Schools and Communities office (in most schools) to speak in your classroom.

Introduction to the Module

Bullying has become a pervasive issue in both schools and the workplace. The victim, the bully, and the environment all suffer from this behavior. Part of the approach to eliminate bullying is helping others understand the issue. If you decide to have peer helpers deliver lessons in their school, it is important to seek prior approval from the teacher or administrator. Review guidelines and share with trainees what is generally appropriate. Have the peer helpers present an interactive lesson, and do follow-up activities. At the end of this module are pre- and postquestionnaires you can give to trainees to use with the lessons.

Communicating With the Teacher Guidelines

Before you present this educational session, it is helpful to meet with the classroom teacher. The following suggestions assume that you will be presenting this session in a classroom, but they may be easily adapted for use in other settings.

1. Introduce yourself and tell why you are participating in this program.
2. Share the goals, objectives, and format of the session, and find out how it fits into the curriculum currently being presented by this teacher.
3. Discuss how the teacher would like you to handle discipline problems, and how you can get help if you become concerned about a student.
4. Set times and dates for the classroom session. Choose an alternative date and time in case the first one doesn't work out. Talk about how much time is actually available and whether or not you have the additional time necessary to conduct supplemental activities.
5. Make sure that you have flip chart paper and easel. If available, an erasable board, smart board, or chalkboard would be helpful.
6. Ask the teacher to give a pre- and postquestionnaire before and after each presentation.

Be careful not to give the impression that you are replacing the teacher during the time you will be in the classroom.

The teacher should remain in the classroom. This will show the students that this is a joint effort. You may require the teacher's assistance with classroom management and coordination. The teacher will also need to reinforce what you teach after you leave. Keep in mind that you are supplementing what the teacher is already doing to prevent bullying. Your message is similar to that of the teacher. Your message strengthens the students' understanding that not only adults, but other students care about them and the choices they make.

Creating a Positive, Interactive Session

Listed below are things to keep in mind when the peer helpers are teaching that can encourage students to take part in the discussions.

1. Maintain proper eye contact with the students.
2. Show respect for their ideas; don't put anyone or their ideas down.
3. Write down what each student says using his or her own words.
4. Reinforce their answers with positive phrases like, "Thanks for your answer," or "That's interesting."
5. Try to call on a variety of students, not just the same few.
6. Use the facilitation skills that encourage helpful attending behavior by asking open-ended questions, paraphrasing, summarizing use of public speaking skills, and large classroom presentations.
7. Consider using interactive games to encourage student involvement.
8. Share your own experiences to help students relate to you personally.

Following Up After Each Presentation

As soon as possible after each presentation, try to set aside some time to meet with the other facilitators, the teacher (if possible), and your peer program professional to review the presentation. This meeting does not need to happen immediately after the presentation, but soon enough to ensure that the experience is still fresh in your mind. One of the most important parts of this program is the opportunity for you to learn from these experiences by discussing them with an adult and the other facilitators. Listed below are questions you could talk about:

1. What parts of the session went well?
2. What did you enjoy about doing the session?
3. What parts were difficult?
4. What could be done next time to make the difficult part easier?
5. What would you do differently to improve the session?
6. What did you learn from the session? About yourself? About your teaching skills? About your students? About your fellow facilitators?
7. Did anything unexpected happen? If so, how did you handle the situation? Are there any other ways you could have handled the situation?

Training Procedures

1. Determine the number of training sessions and exercises to be included in this module.
2. Review the content to be covered, and the suggested activities as listed in *Peer Power, Book Two, Workbook*.
3. You may want to use http://www.stopbullyingnow.hrsa.gov.
4. You may want to use the preassessment before starting this module, and the postassessment at a later time. You may also want the peer helpers to use the pre- and postassessment with others.

Evaluation Process

You can evaluate the process used in teaching a skill by the feedback obtained from the trainees, and by observing their written work and behavior when practicing a presentation on bullying.

Use the J.10 reflections exercise included in the CD in *Peer Programs* when you ask the trainees to write about their reaction. This is a good model to follow. During this module, try to get the peer helpers to sign a pledge card related to bullying prevention.

Measuring Outcomes

1. Use the pre- and post-assessment tool.
2. Use written homework.

EXERCISE 25.1
WHAT IS BULLYING?

Goal

To teach trainees about bullying and the prevalence of bullying

Introduction to the Exercise

If time permits, show *Stop Bullying Now* (see http://www.stopbullyingnow.hrsa.gov), along with conducting the prequestionnaire.

Training Procedures

1. Review the information on bullying. Tailor your remarks to the environment: schools or workplace. You may want to present this as a PowerPoint presentation.
2. Lead a discussion related to the questions at the end of the exercise (1 through 4).
3. Ask the students to discuss their experience with bullying.

Application for Trainees After the Group Meeting

1. Have trainees write down their reaction to Exercise 25.1 and the application information.
2. Have trainees prepare for Exercise 25.2.

EXERCISE 25.2
EFFECTS OF BULLYING ON ME

Goals

To help the trainees understand how bullying affects them

To help trainees recognize bullying in others

Introduction to the Exercise

Research indicates that bullying has a long-term impact. If some of your trainees checked five or more, you may want to meet with them individually to see if they want to be referred to a mental health professional.

Training Procedures

1. Review the reactions to Exercise 25.1 and debrief on that exercise.

2. Ask trainees to write and discuss examples of when they might have been bullied or observed bullying in others.

3. Complete the checklist. If there are five or more checks, meet with them individually to suggest a referral to a mental health professional.

4. Ask the trainees to observe behavior of others and identify if they believe there is any bullying behavior involved.

Application of Trainees After the Group Meeting

1. Have trainees write in a journal their reactions to this exercise with an emphasis on personal experience with bullying (either as victim or bully).

2. Have them prepare for Exercise 25.3.

EXERCISE 25.3
HELPING OTHERS WITH BULLYING

Goals

To train the peer helpers in developing ideas of how to help victims, the bully, and the environment

To help the trainees plan and implement strategies to reduce bullying

Introduction to the Exercise

As you begin to think about how to help others, the focus needs to be on the victim, the bully, and the environment. Work with the peer helpers to plan a policy adoption, and how to help others.

Training Procedures

1. Review reactions from Exercise 25.2.
2. Ask trainees to review ideas to help the victims, bully, and the environment.
3. Divide the trainees into groups of two to discuss how we might help others that are the victim, bully, and the environment.
4. Plan strategies to help reduce bullying. If your peer helpers present classroom lessons or workplace lessons, use the pre- and post-assessment at the end.

Application for Trainees After the Group Meeting

1. Have trainees write in a journal their reactions to Exercise 25.3.
2. Have trainees prepare for Exercise 26.1.

Bullying Reduction

Prequestionnaire

Directions: Please answer the following questions and return to your teacher.

	Yes	Sometimes	No	Comments
1. I know what bullying is.				
2. I know how bullying impacts people.				
3. I know examples of bullying.				
4. I know how bullying has impacted me.				
5. I know how to help stop bullying.				

Name: _____ Date: _____

Grade: _____ Gender: Male: _____ Female: _____

Bullying Reduction

Postquestionnaire

Directions: Please answer the following questions and return to your teacher.

	Yes	Sometimes	No	Comments
1. I know what bullying is.				
2. I know how bullying impacts people.				
3. I know examples of bullying.				
4. I know how bullying has impacted me.				
5. I know how to help stop bullying.				

Name: _____ Date: _____

Grade: _____ Gender: Male: _____ Female: _____

MODULE

PEER HELPING THROUGH MENTORING

Goal

To help the trainees understand mentoring

Approximate Time

Module Introduction—30 minutes

Exercise 26.1—60 to 90 minutes in training session
Application—15 to 30 minutes

Exercise 26.2—30 to 60 minutes in training session
Application—15 minutes

Exercise 26.3—15 to 30 minutes in training session
Application—15 minutes

Exercise 26.4—15 to 30 minutes in training session
Application—15 minutes

Exercise 26.5—60 to 90 minutes in training session
Application—15 minutes

Materials

- *Peer Power, Book Two, Workbook* (one copy for each trainee)
- Optional: Show DVD or CD on mentoring.

Introduction to the Module

It may be beneficial to show trainees a CD or DVD on mentoring. The focus of the presentation should be on the group that you are trying to target. For example, use a DVD that applies to the workplace or schools.

Training Procedures

1. Review the information related to mentoring. Tailor your remarks to schools or the workplace. Select materials that are appropriate for your program and age group.
2. It is important that trainees identify the mentors in their lives. Some youth will indicate they do not have a mentor. Offer an example of a movie or TV show that demonstrates mentor.
3. Develop your program for upper elementary youth helping younger youth; upper grade peer helpers helping ninth graders; older college students helping incoming freshmen, or experienced workers helping new hires.
4. This module should be taught only after trainees have been trained in *Peer Power, Book One*, especially Module V: Attending, Module VI: Empathy, Module VIII: Questioning, Module X: Assertiveness, and Module XII: Problem Solving and Strategy Development 1. Depending on how you will utilize the mentors, you will want to also use *Peer Power, Book Two*, Module XVIII: Peer Helping Through Tutoring, Module XXVIII: Character Education, Module XV: Taking Care of You, or other appropriate modules.
5. Use the J.6 mentor evaluation forms (Mentor Evaluation by the Mentees; Mentor Self-Evaluation, Pre; Mentor Self-Evaluation, Post; Evaluation of Teacher by Mentee; and Evaluation of Parent of Mentor), included in the CD in *Peer Programs*.

Evaluation Process

You can evaluate the process used in teaching a skill by the trainee feedback, and by observation of their written work and behavior when mentoring others.

Use the J.6 mentor evaluation forms (Mentor Evaluation by the Mentees; Mentor Self-Evaluation, Pre; Mentor Self-Evaluation, Post; Evaluation of Teacher by Mentee; and Evaluation of Parent of Mentor) included in the CD in *Peer Programs*.

Exercise 26.4 is a good guide for self-reflection and evaluation.

Measuring Outcomes

1. Use J.6 from the CD in *Peer Programs*
2. Use written application reactions.
3. Prepare for Exercise 26.1.

EXERCISE 26.1
MY MENTOR

Goal

To help trainees become aware of the mentors in their lives

Introduction to the Exercise

This activity can be very powerful for trainees who want to connect with their mentor. Using music from other relaxation activities that you have previously completed may be beneficial to trainees. The drawings and checklist are designed to help access a variety of learning approaches.

Training Procedures

1. Review the introduction to Module XXVI.
2. It is important that trainees identify the mentors in their lives. Some youth will indicate that they do not have a

mentor. Offer an example of a movie or TV show that would provide a mentor role.

3. Ask trainees to relax, play some soft music, and use the following script or one that you have developed.

Be very quiet. Let your mind become quiet; let your body become quiet. Just think about relaxing every muscle and bone in your body. As you become more relaxed go back in time and think about when a friend, a parent, coworker, or relative was a mentor to you. Get that picture clearly in mind. (Pause.) Listen to what this person is saying and feel this person's presence. You might be an observer and see how the mentor looked at you, what the behaviors were, how that felt, and in what way it helped you. (Pause.) As you are imagining the time with your mentor, I would like for you to go and just sit there with your mentor in the sun. Allow the warmth to surround both of you. When you are finished, I would like for you to open your eyes and feel refreshed and relaxed.

4. Ask trainees to picture their mentor and answer the questions.

5. Ask trainees to complete the checklist and answer the questions at the end of the exercise.

6. Put examples on a whiteboard or a flip chart. List characteristics that are offered by the trainees.

Application for Trainees After the Group Meeting

1. Have trainees write down their reaction to Exercise 26.1.
2. Have them prepare for Exercise 26.2.

EXERCISE 26.2
MY PEER HELPING ROLE AS A MENTOR

Goals

To help the trainees understand their role as a mentor

To help trainees understand how they fit into the system

Introduction to the Exercise

As the peer program professional, your job is to have local guidelines copied for the trainees and to be able to develop the "Rules for the Organization and Mentoring." You can also add your own local procedures and responsibilities as the rules can be expanded, if necessary. You may also want to refer to *Peer Power, Book One,* Module SD1: Knowing Your Limits Through Ethical Guidelines as you develop the rules for your organization.

Training Procedures

1. Review the reactions to Exercise 26.1 and debrief on that exercise.

2. Review the mentor role. Discuss what responsibilities a mentor accepts. Ask the trainees to sign and agree to the role of a mentor. Review what the mentor role is not.

3. Review the rules of your organization and ask the trainees to write the organization rule. You may want them to teach each other about the rules once you have reviewed them.

4. Ask them to complete the "when and where" for the procedures required and the responsibilities of mentoring.

Application for Trainees After the Group Meeting

1. Have trainees describe in a journal the reaction to this exercise; emphasize any issues there might be with the guidelines and responsibilities.

2. Have trainees prepare for Exercise 26.3.

EXERCISE 26.3
DEVELOPING A RELATIONSHIP
WITH MY MENTEE

Goals

To train the peer helpers in how to meet with their mentee

To teach trainees how to develop a relationship with the mentee

To show trainees how to plan activities for the mentee

Introduction to the Exercise

This exercise provides the mentor practice on how to meet with a mentee and how to spend time with the mentee.

Training Procedures

1. Review reactions from Exercise 26.2.
2. Ask trainees to review how to develop a mentee relationship, cope with resistance, and what activities to do with the mentee.
3. Divide trainees into groups of three, and ask each person to practice introducing themselves to the others in the group. Practice until everyone has a chance to introduce themselves. Have trainees explain their role as a mentor in the organization and discuss their decision and commitment to be alcohol and drug free.
4. Plan activities to do with their mentee.

Application for Trainees After the Group Meeting

1. Have trainees describe in a journal the reaction to Exercise 26.3.
2. Have trainees prepare for Exercise 26.4.

EXERCISE 26.4
HOW DID THINGS GO?

Goal

To train the peer helpers and mentees in how to keep track of what occurred during the mentoring process

Introduction to the Exercise

This exercise helps track the effectiveness of the mentoring process. You may want to keep track of all reflections, as well as the other forms utilized.

Training Procedures

1. Review reactions from Exercise 26.3.
2. Ask trainees to complete the reflections after they start mentoring.
3. Ask the mentees to complete the reflections after they have been mentored.
4. Assist the mentors with any issues they are having. Ask them to complete an evaluation each time they mentor.

Application for Trainees After the Group Meeting

1. Have trainees record in their journal the reaction to Exercise 26.4.
2. Have trainees prepare for Exercise 26.5.

EXERCISE 26.5
MENTORING REFLECTIONS

Goals

To train the peer helpers in the process of reflection

To help the trainees internalize the experience of mentoring others

Introduction to the Exercise

Research has indicated the importance of reflection to truly integrate beliefs and behavior. This is the final segment of learning helping behaviors.

Training Procedures

1. Discuss Exercise 26.4.

2. Request the trainees to answer the questions in Exercise 26.5.

3. Ask them to discuss this with the whole group.

4. Use this on a regular basis while they are mentoring.

Application for Trainees After the Group Meeting

Have trainees prepare for Module XXVII.

MODULE XXVII

A PEER HELPER'S ROLE IN CRISIS MANAGEMENT

Goal

To help trainees understand their role in crisis management

Approximate Time

Module Introduction—15 minutes

Exercise 27.1—30 to 60 minutes in training session
Application—15 to 30 minutes

Exercise 27.2—30 to 60 minutes in training session
Application—15 minutes

Exercise 27.3—30 to 60 minutes in training session
Application—15 minutes

Exercise 27.4—60 to 90 minutes in training session
Application—15 minutes

Materials

- *Peer Power, Book Two, Workbook* (one copy for each trainee)

Introduction to the Module

Peer helpers are a valuable resource in providing crisis management during natural or other kinds of disasters. Their role is to provide appropriate referrals and support the professional handling the disaster. If you utilize peer helpers in any role in a crisis, it is important to debrief them after the activity to protect their own well-being.

Training Procedures

1. Select materials that are appropriate for your program.
2. Peer helpers can assist in crises such as hurricanes, floods, loss of electricity, and shootings. The peer helpers should have completed this module, as well as know how to deal with loss covered, which are topics covered in Module XXIII: Coping with Loss and Module XV: Taking Care of You! Stress Management.
3. This module is appropriate for high school and college students and adult populations. The module should be taught only after trainees have been trained in *Peer Power, Book One*, especially Module V: Attending, Module VI: Empathy, and Module VIII: Questioning.
4. Use the J.10 for self-reflection included in the CD in *Peer Programs*.

Evaluation Process

You can evaluate the process used in teaching a skill by the trainee feedback and by observation of their written work and behavior when mentoring others in a crisis situation.

Measuring Outcomes

1. Use J.10 from the CD in *Peer Programs*
2. Use your own observations.
3. Use the checklist in Exercise 27.3.

EXERCISE 27.1
WHAT IS A POTENTIALLY TRAUMATIZING EVENT?

Goals

To teach the trainees what is a potentially traumatizing event

To show trainees how to manage potentially traumatizing events

Introduction to the Exercise

This activity can be a very powerful tool for trainees to review different kinds of crises. This exercise can bring back memories and sometimes sadness.

Training Procedures

1. Review the introduction to this module. Lead a discussion about the issues described in the introduction.
2. Review potentially traumatizing events.
3. Discuss other possible causes of trauma.
4. Have trainees read the checklist of traumatizing events and check any they have experienced. If any of the trainees checks several, you may want to meet with them individually.
5. Be sensitive to those who have been through much trauma. Suggest that they not go through the training.
6. Discuss coping tools used to deal with these events.

Application for Trainees After the Group Meeting

1. Have trainees write down their reaction to Exercise 27.1.
2. Have trainees prepare for Exercise 27.2.

EXERCISE 27.2
RECOGNIZING SIGNS OF POSTTRAUMATIC STRESS DISORDER (PTSD) AND STRESS DISORDER

Goals

To teach trainees the human response to crisis

To teach trainees how to recognize the warning signs to stress

To help trainees be able to identify the signs of PTSD

To teach trainees how to recognize human response to trauma

To give trainees practice referring those impacted to a mental health professional

Introduction to the Exercise

This exercise will provider trainees with practice in making a referral based on information learned in Exercise 25.1.

Training Procedures

1. Ask trainees to review the typical adult response to crisis and how it differs from children's responses.

2. Ask trainees to review and discuss the warning signs of stress.

3. Ask trainees to review the signs indicating different stages of PTSD and discuss the human response signs to trauma.

4. Ask trainees to take the assessment of PTSD, either for themselves or someone they know. If anyone has checked over five of these, you may wish to meet with them individually. You may also want to refer them to a mental health professional.

5. Ask trainees to practice referring others to a mental health professional. Work in groups of three, with one person taking the role of the helper, one the helpee, and one the observer. Rotate until everyone has a chance to practice each role.

Application of Trainees After the Group Meeting

1. Have trainees describe in a journal your reaction to this exercise. Emphasize any issues related to helping others in a crisis situation.
2. Have trainees prepare for Exercise 27.3.

EXERCISE 27.3
DEFINITIONS

Goals

To help trainees learn multiple definitions in crisis management

To learn their role in the process

To have trainees practice helping others in crisis

Introduction to the Exercise

This exercise often involves more than one training session. It is important that the trainees have an opportunity to practice what they have learned. The observer will need to use the observer checklist to be effective.

Training Procedures

1. Ask trainees to review the definitions and lead a discussion.
2. Define the role of the peer helper based on your program guidelines.
3. Use the scenarios to have peer helpers improvise a practice session, which will show how to actually talk to a younger child, coworker, or friend who has recently experienced a disaster. The assumption is that the peer helper is referring the person to a crisis management professional. The scenario also presumes that the peer helper is talking with someone who is upset. Make sure the peer helpers understand that they also need to make the person feel comfortable physically (water, etc.).

4. Divide into groups of three. Assign roles of peer helper, helpee, and observer. Observers will use the checklist to record the skills noted. Spend about 5 minutes on each scenario. Change roles and repeat until all have had a chance to play each of the roles.

5. Ask the trainees to write about their reaction to Exercise 27.3.

Application for Trainees After the Group Meeting

1. Have trainees describe in a journal the reaction to Exercise 27.3.

2. Have trainees review the checklists and think about how to improve the practice session.

3. Have them prepare for Exercise 27.4.

EXERCISE 27.4
CRITICAL ISSUES IN PEER HELPING PROVIDING CRISIS MANAGEMENT

Goals

To help trainees learn how to apply the information learned

To teach trainees problem-solving tools for crisis management

Introduction to the Exercise

During this exercise, trainees will apply what they have learned in this module. They will teach others about the issues and discuss how to solve crisis management dilemmas.

Training Procedures

1. Set up teams of three. Allow each team 15 minutes to plan for a 15-minute presentation on the topics listed in the *Peer Power, Book Two, Workbook*.

2. Make sure every one is involved and uses presentation skills, along with visual aids.

3. You may want to review Module XIX: Peer Helping Through Group Work: Peer Education and Support.

4. Have an observer give feedback on the group presentation.

Application for Trainees After the Group Meeting

1. Have trainees describe in a journal the reaction to Exercise 27.4.

2. Have trainees prepare for Exercise 28.1.

MODULE XXVIII

PEER HELPING THROUGH CHARACTER EDUCATION DEVELOPMENT

Goal

To help trainees learn how to develop positive character traits in youth

Approximate Time

Module Introduction—15 minutes

Exercise 28.1—60 to 90 minutes in training session
Application—30 to 60 minutes

Exercise 28.2—30 to 60 minutes in training session
Application—15 minutes

Exercise 28.3—30 to 60 minutes in training session
Application—30 minutes

Exercise 28.4—60 to 90 minutes in training session
Application—15 minutes

Exercise 28.5—60 to 90 minutes in training session

Application—15 minutes

Exercise 28.6—30 to 60 minutes in training session

Application—15 minutes

Exercise 28.7—30 to 60 minutes in training session

Application—15 minutes

Materials

- *Peer Power, Book Two, Workbook* (one copy for each trainee)

Introduction to the Module

Character development is crucial to becoming a good citizen. These exercises will assist the trainee in developing positive character traits. You may want the peer helpers to take these lessons into their classrooms. These lessons are recommended for high school age students. It may be beneficial to review lessons for younger youth. This module is most effective when the peer helpers teach these lessons to others.

The steps outlined in Exercise 28.1 are helpful for use with each of the exercises. Review *Peer Power, Book Two, Workbook* and Module XIX: Group Work. The following are guidelines to use within the classroom.

Communicating With the Teacher Guidelines

Before you present this session, it is helpful to meet with the classroom teacher. The following ideas assume that you will be presenting this session in a classroom, but they may be easily adapted for use in other settings:

1. Introduce yourself and tell why you are participating in a character education program.
2. Share the goals, objectives, and format of the session and find out how it fits into the curriculum currently being presented by this teacher.

3. Discuss how the teacher would like you to handle discipline problems and how you can get help if you become concerned about a student.

4. Set times and dates for the classroom session. Choose an alternative date and time in case the first one doesn't work out. Discuss how much time is actually available, and if you have the additional time necessary to conduct supplemental activities.

5. Make sure you have flip chart paper and an easel. If available, an erasable board, smart board, or chalkboard would be helpful.

6. Ask the teacher to give a pre- and postquestionnaire before and after each presentation.

Be careful not to give the impression that you are replacing the teacher during the time you will be in the classroom. The teacher should remain in the classroom. This will show the students that this is a joint effort. You may require the teacher's assistance with classroom management and coordination. The teacher will also need to reinforce what you teach after you leave. Keep in mind that you are supplementing what the teacher is already teaching in character education. Your message is similar to that of the teacher. You message strengthens the students' understanding that not only adults, but other students care about them and the choices they make.

Creating a Positive, Interactive Session

Listed below are things to keep in mind when the peer helpers are teaching; these can encourage students to take part in the discussions.

1. Maintain proper eye contact with the students.

2. Show respect for their ideas; don't put anyone or any ideas down.

3. Write down what each student says using his or her own words.

4. Reinforce their answers with positive phrases like, "Thanks for your answer," or "That's interesting."

5. Try to call on a variety of students, not just the same few.

6. Use the facilitation skills that encourage attending behavior by asking open-ended questions, paraphrasing, summarizing, public speaking skills, and large classroom presentations.

7. Share your own experiences to help students relate to you, personally.

Following Up After Each Presentation

As soon as possible after each presentation, try to set aside some time to meet with the other facilitators, the teacher (if possible), and your peer program professional to review the presentation. This meeting does not need to happen immediately after the presentation, but soon enough to ensure that the experience is still fresh in your mind. One of the most important parts of this program is the opportunity for you to learn from these experiences by discussing them with an adult and the other facilitators. Listed below are questions you could talk about:

1. What parts of the session went well?

2. What did you enjoy about doing the session?

3. What parts were difficult?

4. What could be done next time to make the difficult parts easier?

5. What would you do differently to improve the session?

6. What did you learn from the session? About yourself? About your teaching skills? About your students? About your fellow facilitators?

7. Did anything unexpected happen? If so, how did you handle the situation? Are there any other ways you could have handled the situation?

Training Procedures

1. Determine materials that are appropriate for your program.

2. If lessons are already in place in your school for character education, you should implement them.

3. This module is appropriate for high school and college students, and adult populations.

4. This module should be taught only after trainees have been trained in *Peer Power, Book One*, especially Module V: Attending, Module VI: Empathy, and Module VIII: Questioning.

5. Use J.10 for self-reflection included in the CD in *Peer Programs*.

Evaluation Process

You can evaluate the process used in teaching a skill by the trainee feedback obtained, and by observation of their written work and behavior when teaching others.

Measuring Outcomes

1. Use J.10 from the CD.
2. Use your own observation.

EXERCISE 28.1
STEPS FOR A CHARACTER EDUCATION TRAINING SESSION

Goals

To teach trainees how to set up character education sessions

To introduce typical character education traits

Introduction to the Exercise

Model the appropriate method to teach character education by demonstrating the steps involved in conducting a session.

Training Procedures

1. Review the introduction to this module. Lead a discussion concerning the need for development of character education traits in themselves and others.

2. Demonstrate the steps involved in teaching a character education session.

3. Review common character education traits and discuss additional traits that need to be developed.

4. Have a discussion with trainees about how to get parents involved in supporting these traits.

Application for Trainees After the Group Meeting

1. Have trainees write their reaction to Exercise 28.1.

2. Have trainees prepare for Exercise 28.2.

**EXERCISE 28.2
RESPONSIBILITY**

Goals

To teach trainees how to facilitate a responsibility lesson

To help the trainees know the importance of fulfilling responsibilities

Introduction to the Exercise

This exercise will assist trainees in learning about responsibility.

Training Procedures

1. Ask the trainees to define responsibility. Record the answers next to "What" on the whiteboard.

2. Ask trainees to determine why responsibility is important. Record their responses next to "Why" on the whiteboard.

3. Lead a discussion regarding when it is important to demonstrate responsibility. Ask for specific examples.

4. Divide the class and ask one team to teach 1, 2, and 3 above to the other team. Reverse roles.

5. Read the Dan story, ask questions, and lead a discussion about their responses.
6. Assign the application to take home to complete and share with their family.

Application of Trainees After the Group Meeting

1. Have trainees answer the questions about responsibilities.
2. Have trainees share their knowledge with their families.
3. Have them prepare for Exercise 28.3.

EXERCISE 28.3
SERVICE (CITIZENSHIP)

Goal

To facilitate a service lesson that leads to good citizenship

Introduction to the Exercise

Service to others is the mark of good citizenship. As trainees are reviewing the scenario, it is important to help them make the connection if they do not do so on their own.

Training Procedures

1. Ask trainees to review the definition on service and lead a discussion on the topic.
2. Read the scenario on Amy.
3. Lead a discussion about Amy and how she should handle her situation.
4. Lead a discussion about community service and plan a community service event.
5. Divide the classroom into two teams. One team presents the service lesson to the other team. Reverse roles.

Application for Trainees After the Group Meeting

1. Have trainees complete a community service project. It could be teaching this lesson to others.
2. Ask trainees to reflect on their thoughts regarding the community service project by writing a paper.
3. Ask trainees to prepare for Exercise 28.4.

EXERCISE 28.4
HONESTY, RESPONSIBILITY

Goals

To help trainees learn how to facilitate honesty through the responsibility lesson

To help trainees understand the importance of being loyal to their family

To help trainees learn how to make responsible decisions

Introduction to the Exercise

During this exercise, trainees will lead a classroom lesson on honesty and responsibility. They can debate the content to be included in the lesson.

Training Procedures

1. Read Seville's problem situation.
2. Lead trainees in the discussion questions.
3. Present the steps in good decision making. Ask trainees to apply these steps to Seville's problem situation.
4. Divide the class in order to practice delivering this lesson.

Application for Trainees After the Group Meeting

1. Ask trainees to apply the decision steps to their personal lives during this week.
2. Have trainees report on their experience with the decision steps at the next training session.

EXERCISE 28.5
HUMANITY, RESPECT

Goals

To teach trainees how to facilitate the humanity, respect lessons

To teach trainees how to facilitate lessons on respecting others' property

Introduction to the Exercise

During this exercise, the trainees will lead a classroom lesson on humanity and respect. They will practice being respectful to others.

Training Procedures

1. Read Jose's problem.
2. Ask the trainees to answer the questions and have a debate, if appropriate.
3. Define respect and give examples.
4. Divide the trainees into teams to practice delivering this lesson to each other.

Application for Trainees After the Group Meeting

1. Have trainees practice being respectful to others.
2. Have trainees report on experiences at the next training session.

EXERCISE 28.6
HONESTY, SELF-ESTEEM

Goal

To learn how to facilitate a lesson on honesty and self esteem, particularly in a relationship

Introduction to the Exercise

During this exercise, trainees will lead a classroom lesson on honesty and self-esteem and apply it to relationships.

Training Procedures

1. Read James's problem.
2. Facilitate a discussion and debate.
3. Lead a discussion regarding how honesty impacts relationships and builds self-esteem.
4. Divide trainees into teams in order to practice delivering this lesson to each other.

Application for Trainees After the Group Meeting

1. Ask trainees to write a story about James and Sue, and use honesty as the focus of the story.
2. Ask trainees to consider how honesty in a relationship builds self-esteem. Have them share their thoughts in writing.
3. Have them write another story about how honesty can help other relationships.

EXERCISE 28.7
HONESTY, RESPECT, PERSEVERANCE, AND GOAL-SETTING

Goal

To teach trainees how to facilitate an honesty, respect, perseverance, and goal-setting lesson to help others learn the importance of telling the truth

Introduction to the Exercise

During this exercise, the trainees will lead a classroom lesson on honesty and respect and apply the lesson to telling the truth.

Training Procedures

1. Read Will's problem.
2. Facilitate a discussion and debate.
3. Lead a discussion that centers around goal setting and how it applies to telling the truth.
4. Divide trainees into teams to practice delivering this lesson to each other.

Application for Trainees After the Group Meeting

1. Ask trainees to write about what they have learned in this module and how it has impacted them personally.
2. Have trainees develop a plan for teaching the lessons to others, and initiate the plan.
3. Ask trainees to write another story about how honesty helps other relationships.

MODULE XXIX

PROBLEM GAMBLING: PREVENTION AND INTERVENTION

Goals

To help trainees learn how to educate others about problem gambling

To teach trainees how to provide intervention to others if needed

Approximate Time

Module Introduction—15 minutes

Exercise 29.1—30 to 60 minutes in training session
Application—15 to 30 minutes

Exercise 29.2—30 to 60 minutes in training session
Application—15 minutes

Exercise 29.3—30 to 60 minutes in training session
Application—30 minutes

Materials

- *Peer Power, Book Two, Workbook* (one copy for each trainee)

Introduction to the Module

Gambling may be a problem in your school or organization. The consequences of gambling can be devastating to individuals and families. It is an issue people have a difficult time talking about and admitting to. Many individuals are embarrassed to discuss issues related to gambling. Education is the first step in helping others see the impact that gambling has on individuals and families. You may want the trainees to use these lessons in their classrooms. This module is recommended for high school and college age students and adult populations.

You may want to review *Peer Power, Book Two, Workbook*, Module XIX: Group Work before you present this module to educational groups and others. The following are guidelines to be used within the classroom.

Communicating With the Teacher Guidelines

Before you present this educational session, it is helpful to meet with the classroom teacher. The following suggestions assume that you will be presenting this session in a classroom, but they may be easily adapted for use in other settings.

1. Introduce yourself and tell why you are participating in this program.
2. Share the goals, objectives, and format of the session, and find out how it fits into the curriculum currently being presented by this teacher.
3. Discuss how the teacher would like you to handle discipline problems and how you can get help if you become concerned about a student.
4. Set times and dates for the classroom session. Choose an alternative date and time in case the first one doesn't work out. Talk about how much time is actually available and whether or not you have the additional time available to conduct supplemental activities.

5. Make sure that you have flip chart paper, and an easel. An erasable board, smart board, or chalkboard would be helpful.
6. Ask the teacher to give a pre- and postquestionnaire before and after each presentation.

Be careful not to give the impression that you are replacing the teacher during the time you will be in the classroom. The teacher should remain in the classroom. This will show the students that this is a joint effort. You may require the teacher's assistance with classroom management and coordination. The teacher will also need to reinforce what you teach after you leave. Keep in mind that you are supplementing what the teacher is already teaching students about problem gambling. Your message is similar to that of the teacher. Your message strengthens the students' understanding that not only adults, but other students care about them and the choices they make.

Creating a Positive, Interactive Session

Listed below are things for the peer helpers to keep in mind when they are teaching; these can encourage students to take part in the discussions.

1. Maintain proper eye contact with the students.
2. Show respect for their ideas: Don't put anyone or any idea down.
3. Write down what each student says using his or her own words.
4. Reinforce their answers with positive phrases like, "Thanks for your answer," or "That's interesting."
5. Try to call on a variety of students, not just the same few.
6. Use the facilitation skills that encourage attending behavior by asking open-ended questions, paraphrasing, summarizing, using public speaking skills, and giving large classroom presentations.
7. Share your own experiences to help students relate to you personally.

Following up After Each Presentation

As soon as possible after each presentation, try to set aside some time to meet with the other facilitators, the teacher (if possible), and your peer program professional to review the presentation. This meeting does not need to happen immediately after the presentation, but soon enough to ensure that the experience is still fresh in your mind. One of the most important parts of this program is the opportunity for you to learn from these experiences by discussing them with a trainer or other facilitators. Listed below are questions you could talk about.

- What parts of the session went well?
- What did you enjoy about doing the session?
- What parts were difficult?
- What could be done next time to make the difficult parts easier?
- What would you do differently to improve the session?
- What did you learn from the session? About yourself? About your teaching skills? About your students? About your fellow facilitators?
- Did anything unexpected happen? If so, how did you handle the situation? Are there any other ways you could have handled the situation?

Training Procedures

1. Select materials that are appropriate for the program.
2. This module is appropriate for high school and college students and for adult populations in general.
3. You may want to have trainees research gambling on the Internet.
4. Use the J.10 for self-reflections included in the CD in *Peer Programs*.

Evaluation Process

You can evaluate the process used in teaching a skill by trainee feedback and by observation of their written work and behavior when teaching others. You will also have a chance to observe the trainees in Exercise 29.3.

Measuring Outcomes

1. Use J.10 from the CD in *Peer Programs*.
2. Use your own observation.

EXERCISE 29.1
WHAT ARE TYPES OF GAMBLING?

Goals

To help the trainees learn about the different types of gambling

To help trainees understand pathological gambling in others

Introduction to the Exercise

It is important for trainees to recognize different types of gambling: problem gambling and pathological gambling. Trainees will need to be able to internalize this information by recognizing the behaviors in themselves or others. Often, they are surprised at the different kinds of gambling.

Training Procedures

1. Review the introduction to this module. Lead a discussion that centers on the need for education about problem gambling and pathological gambling.
2. Make sure they understand the difference concerning problem gambling and pathological gambling.
3. Lead a discussion regarding signs of problem gambling.
4. Have trainees respond to the questions at the end of the exercise and lead a discussion centered on the questions.

Application for Trainees After the Group Meeting

1. Have the trainees write down their reaction to Exercise 29.1.
2. Have trainees prepare for Exercise 29.2.

EXERCISE 29.2
PROBLEM GAMBLING SELF-TEST FOR TEENS

Goals

To help trainees understand the issues related to teen gambling

To teach trainees how to use the self-test

Introduction to the Exercise

This exercise will show trainees how to conduct self-evaluations and to understand how to use the information to help others.

Training Procedures

1. Ask the trainees to define problem gambling, as discussed in Exercise 29.1.
2. Ask the trainees to answer the questions for the "A Self-Test for Teens." If trainees have seven or more yes answers (positive responses), you may want to meet with them to discuss a possible referral to a mental health professional.
3. Lead a discussion about how to use the test with others.
4. Lead a discussion about how to help others with problem gambling. Your group may want to give educational lessons to others, FACT sheets, posters, etc.

Application of Trainees After the Group Meeting

1. Have trainees answer the questions related to the exercise.
2. Ask them to write a reaction to Exercise 29.2.
3. Have trainees prepare for Exercise 29.3 by researching resources on the Internet listed in Exercise 29.3.

EXERCISE 29.3
PRACTICE HELPING OTHERS WITH GAMBLING ISSUES

Goals

To practice helping others with gambling issues

To learn how to refer those with problem gambling to a mental health professional

Training Procedures

1. Ask for reactions to Exercise 29.2 and what was learned from the Internet.
2. Divide trainees into groups of three. One person will play the helper, one the helpee, and one the observer. Ask the observer to look at helping and referral skills.

Application for Trainees After the Group Meeting

1. Ask trainees to reflect by writing about the practice exercise and how they can use what they have learned to help others.
2. Have trainees review the introduction to Module XXX.

MODULE XXX

YOUTH TOBACCO PREVENTION THROUGH COMMUNITY IMPACT

Goals

To help trainees learn about the impact of tobacco use

To show trainees how they can assist the community in smoking less or becoming smoke-free

Approximate Time

Module Introduction—10 minutes

Exercise 30.1—30 to 60 minutes in training session

Application—30 to 60 minutes

Exercise 30.2—30 to 60 minutes in training session

Application—60 to 90 minutes

Exercise 30.3—30 to 60 minutes in training session

Application—90 to 120 minutes

Exercise 30.4—30 to 60 minutes in training session

Application—60 to 90 minutes

Materials

- *Peer Power, Book Two, Workbook* (one copy for each trainee)

Introduction to the Module

Tobacco is the single greatest avoidable cause of disease and death. Peer helpers can be a part of helping others become educated about tobacco use. Peer helpers can also be effective in changing policies and practices in the organization and community. This module is an opportunity to become involved in a major health issue and put strategies into action, such as influencing local establishments to become smoke free, impacting legislation related to tobacco issues, and other changes in the community. Classroom and workplace presentations are also very helpful.

Review *Peer Power, Book Two, Workbook*, Module XIX: Group Work before you deliver this session to educational groups and others.

Training Procedures

1. Review the module to determine the focus of your training and select exercises that fit your program.
2. This module is appropriate for high school and college students and adult populations.
3. Have trainees use the Internet to research tobacco use, secondhand smoke, and advocacy of community efforts to become a smoke-free environment.
4. Use J.10 for self-reflection included in the CD in *Peer Programs*.
5. Invite speakers from your local Cancer Society, American Lung Association, or other appropriate agencies to address the trainees.

Evaluation Process

You can evaluate the process used in teaching about the impact of tobacco and how to advocate for a healthier environment by trainee feedback, and by observation of their written work and behavior when teaching the information to others. You will also have a chance to observe the trainees during their involvement in community projects.

Measuring Outcomes

1. Use J.10 from the CD in *Peer Programs*.
2. Use your own observation.

EXERCISE 30.1
TOBACCO ISSUES

Goal

To help trainees understand the impact of tobacco use on smokers, as well as the effects of secondhand smoke

Introduction to the Exercise

It is important for the trainees to become educated about the impact of tobacco use on smokers, the effects of secondhand smoke, and of youth and tobacco use. Trainees need to have the opportunity to learn more about the issue by visiting various local agencies and by researching current tobacco facts from the Internet. You may also have the peer helpers teach others about the issue.

Training Procedures

1. Review the introduction to this module. Lead a discussion about the need for education concerning the impact of tobacco use by individuals and the effects of secondhand smoke.
2. Trainees should be able to understand major issues related to tobacco uses.
3. Lead a discussion about tobacco use among teens.

4. Have trainees respond to the questions at the end of the exercise.

5. Invite an expert speaker to talk about the impact of tobacco on society.

Application for Trainees After the Group Meeting

1. Have the trainees write down their reaction to Exercise 30.1.
2. Have trainees prepare for Exercise 30.2.

EXERCISE 30.2
TOBACCO MARKETS TO YOUTH

Goal

To raise awareness of how the tobacco industry markets to youth

Introduction to the Exercise

The tobacco industry spends a lot of money on marketing tobacco use to young people. This exercise is important for youth to recognize how tobacco companies target them by advertising through magazines, supermarkets, quick shops, and so on.

Training Procedures

1. Ask the trainees to discuss the impact of tobacco use by youth.
2. Ask the trainees to report what they have learned from observing advertisements in stores, on billboards, and so on.
3. Lead a discussion concerning what they have learned by looking at magazines about tobacco use.
4. Have trainees learn about state and local policies regarding smoking in public places and the laws in the state concerning youth and smoking.
5. Ask the trainees to consider what kind of advocacy role they could practice concerning tobacco use.

Application of Trainees After the Group Meeting

1. Ask trainees to answer the questions about the exercise.
2. Ask trainees to write their reaction to Exercise 30.2.
3. Have them prepare for Exercise 30.3 by researching resources at both the state and local level, and on the Internet.

EXERCISE 30.3
IMPACTING THE COMMUNITY: PREVENTION OF TOBACCO USE OF YOUTH

Goal

To practice becoming advocates for smoke-free or smoke-fewer communities through surveying tools

Introduction to the Exercise

This is an opportunity for youth to learn how to advocate for a healthier environment through survey tools and by educating local establishments and local city councils about the impact of smoking on the environment.

Training Procedures

1. Ask trainees for their reaction to Exercise 30.2 and what they have learned from the Internet and other sources.
2. Divide the trainees into groups of three. Practice talking to a local restaurant owner advocating for a smoke-free environment.
3. Work with the trainees to develop survey questions, and develop a plan to survey at least 100 people on their opinion about smoke-free public places and so on. Ask questions related to consequences of becoming a smoke-free community. Your state and community may already have a policy; therefore, you may want to focus on advertising in commercial establishments. Tailor your survey to issues in your community.

4. Talk to retail establishments about becoming smoke free or about not advertising tobacco in their business.

5. Discuss the activities when completed.

Application for Trainees After the Group Meeting

1. Ask trainees to reflect through writing about the exercise and how they might help others.

2. Ask trainees to review Exercise 30.4.

EXERCISE 30.4
STRATEGIES TO HELP YOUTH STAY TOBACCO-FREE

Goals

To teach trainees strategies to help youth stay tobacco-free

To help trainees develop a plan of action to implement the strategies

Introduction to the Exercise

This is an opportunity to teach peer helpers how to develop a campaign to assist the environment to become smoke free. It is important to not just plan, but to implement these strategies.

Training Procedures

1. Brainstorm ideas that they would like to see implemented concerning education, policies, and advocacy related to smoking, particularly in youth.

2. Review the ideas listed in the workbook and research other ideas.

3. Complete the plan of action for the activities.

4. Implement the activities.

5. Reflect on the experience.

6. Remember to have them practice first before doing the activities.

Application for Trainees After the Group Meeting

1. Ask trainees to reflect through writing about the exercise, and how they might help others.

2. Ask trainees to complete the self-evaluation in the workbook and discuss it with you on an individual basis.

ADDITIONAL RESOURCES

Tindall, J. (2008). *Peer Power, Book One, Strategies for the Professional Leader: Becoming an Effective Peer Helper and Conflict Mediator.* Boca Raton, FL: Taylor & Francis Group.

Tindall, J. (2008). *Peer Power, Book One, Workbook: Becoming an Effective Peer Helper and Conflict Mediator.* Boca Raton, FL: Taylor & Francis Group.

Tindall, J. (2008). *Peer Power, Book Two, Workbook: Applying Peer Helper Skills.* Boca Raton, FL: Taylor & Francis Group.

Tindall, J. & Black, D. R. (2008). *Peer Programs: An In-Depth Look at Peer Programs: Planning, Implementation, and Administration.* Bristol, PA: Taylor & Francis.

Tindall, J. & Salmon, S. (1993). *Feelings: The 3 Rs—Receiving, Reflecting, Responding.* Muncie, IN: Accelerated Development.

Tindall, J. & Salmon-White, S. (1990). *Peers Helping Peers: Program for the Preadolescent, Leader Manual.* Muncie, IN: Accelerated Development.

Tindall, J. & Salmon-White, S. (1990). *Peers Helping Peers: Program for the Preadolescent, Student Workbook.* Muncie, IN: Accelerated Development.

ADDITIONAL
RESOURCES

AUTHOR

Judith A. Tindall, PhD

Judith A. Tindall, PhD, is president of Psychological Network, Inc., a full-service psychological group in St. Charles, Missouri. She is currently licensed as a psychologist and professional counselor. She holds certifications as a teacher, school counselor, National Association of Peer Programs (NAPP) trainer/consultant, Certified Peer Program Educator, Myers–Briggs Type Inventory (MBTI®)-certified trainer, and custody evaluator. She has been in private practice in St. Charles since the late 1970s. She has been a consultant at the local, state, national, and international level for both public and private organizations, associations, hospitals, schools, social service agencies, and the faith community. She has assisted those organizations on a wide variety of topics, including peer programs, safety, strategic planning, team building, leadership development, executive coaching, communication skills, care for the caregiver, total quality management, stress management, violence prevention, sexual harassment, diversity and MBTI®, community-building, HIV-AIDS, compulsive gambling, and other topics.

She has recently been elected vice president of the National Organizations for Youth Safety (NOYS), which is a collaborative organization made up of 40 youth-serving organizations. She also serves on the board of directors of NAPP, BACCHUS Peer Education Network, services for higher education, advocating for health and safety.

Some recent highlights of her work with peer programs are working with the National Highway Traffic Safety Administration (NHTSA) in evaluating projects on zero tolerance for underage drinking and driving and bike safety; helping the Future Farmers of America in creating a national evaluation model for its programs; consulting with the United Nations to develop and implement an international peer program and crisis management program (staff outreach support providers); and working with the Department of Education in Indiana and with Kansas City public schools regarding creating, enhancing, and evaluating peer programs. She currently leads her group in providing mental health services to St. Louis Job Corps. She has trained and consulted with thousands of adults internationally in a variety of peer programs and trained over 20,000 youth and adults in peer-delivered activities such as peer helping, mediation, leadership, tutoring, crisis management, traffic safety, health, and group work.

Prior to this, she worked in public schools for 18 years as a teacher, counselor, and guidance director. She has taught courses at the graduate level at the University of Missouri-St. Louis, Webster University, and Lindenwood University. Those courses included group process, assessment of the individual, multicultural counseling, and other courses. Typical of her ENTJ (MBTI®), she has been an officer in local, state, and national professional organizations and volunteer organizations. She is past president of St. Charles Sunrise Rotary, National Peace Institute, National Peer Helpers Association, Missouri Peer Helpers Association, and Missouri Counselors Association; secretary for St. Louis Psychological Association; and vice president of the American School Counselors Association. She has received various recognitions from professional associations such as the National Peer Helpers Association Scholar of the Year and the Barbara Varenhorst Award of Merit, Missouri Counselors Association (MCA) distinguished service award, Harry S. Duncan Missouri Peer Helpers Association

(MPHA) award, Missouri Mental Health Counselors Association (MMHCA) association merit award, and St. Charles Sunrise Rotarian of the Year.

She has written many books: *Peer Program: An In-Depth Look at Peer Programs: Planning, Implementation, and Administration; Peer Power, Book One, Strategies for the Professional Leader: Becoming an Effective Peer Helper and Conflict Mediator; Peer Power, Book One, Workbook: Becoming an Effective Peer Helper and Conflict Mediator; Peer Power, Book Two, Strategies for the Professional Leader: Applying Peer Helper Skills; Peer Power, Book Two, Workbook: Applying Peer Helper Skills; Peers Helping Peers: Program for the Preadolescent and Leader's Manual;* and *Feelings: The 3 Rs—Receiving, Reflecting, Responding.* She has written many referred journal articles and for the popular press, including *St. Louis Business Journal* and *St. Charles Business Magazine.* She has also appeared on radio and television, including *Good Morning America.*

Dr. Tindall has a PhD in psychology from St. Louis University; Specialist from Southern Illinois University, Edwardsville in counseling and psychology; MEd from University of Missouri at Columbia; and a BS in education from Southwest Minnesota State University in Speech and Political Science. She is married, has two sons, and enjoys playing golf, spending time with friends, and reading. She is also a St. Louis Cardinals and St. Louis University Billikens fan.